Essential Leadership Skills for Hospitality Supervisors:

An Experiential Approach

GEORGE OJIE-AHAMIOJIE

authorHOUSE®

AuthorHouse™
1663 Liberty Drive, Suite 200
Bloomington, IN 47403
www.authorhouse.com
Phone: 1-800-839-8640

First published by AuthorHouse 7/25/2008

ISBN: 978-1-4389-0104-6 (sc)

Printed in the United States of America
Bloomington, Indiana

This book is printed on acid-free paper.

DEDICATION

This book is dedicated to all the men and women of this noble hospitality industry. This is the industry where we work on weekends and holidays while everyone plays, work long hours while everyone relaxes, and provide excellent and high quality customer/ guest service in the face of so many challenges and adversities.

I salute all of you. I hope you keep your passion glowing and your dedication to providing quality product and services unalloyed!

Acknowledgement

Many thanks to friends and family members who have always encourage me to explore writing and publication. In addition, thank you goes to those individuals who have always come to me for my opinions whenever they have challenges at work, with their peers, and or with their supervisors.

I hope this book will provide that avenue for you to explore ways to lead the employees in your organization, relate to everyone on an individual basis, and realize that we are in the people's business.

Finally, to my family whom I owe my life. My lovely wife Maria and the three Angels: Princess Britnie, Precious Kortnie, and Pebble Whitnie. I live and love because of you.

The success of any organization, is a direct link to the employees' performance. In the hospitality industry, several managers work long hours; five to six days a week, with little or no quality of life. So the success of these supervisors is not only important, but necessary. The fact is their success is directly linked to their employees' performance. And the employees will only provide high-quality service when they feel the managers are on their side and have provided the tools, training, and motivation necessary for them to be productive employees. Due to the intense labor of this industry and the continued changing of the workforce, supervisors must learn how to effectively communicate, train, develop, delegate, and motivate this diverse workforce. They must also learn how to handle marginal employees, solve problems, and make good and effective decisions.

Essential Leadership Skills for Hospitality Supervisor – An Experiential Approach, will help you in the acquisition of the knowledge, skills, and abilities necessary to succeed in this endeavor. This book will not only discuss several theories and concepts, but will also provide you with several practical applications you will need to be successful.

This book is easy to read and understand. It teaches you how to select the best talents in your team, train, develop, and motivate these employees; how to empower and delegate some of your responsibilities; how to provide the tools needed to accomplish the tasks; and finally how to move from a manager who **does things right**, to ultimate become a leader who **does the right things right!**

I hope you find this book motivating and helpful. I wish you continued success in your career and this industry!

CONTENTS

CHAPTER ONE

Leadership

*"Leaders are best when no one know they exist; not at
their best when people obey and compliments them;
worse when they are despised by the people. However,
leaders who talk little, when their work is done and their
goal fulfilled, people will say 'we did it by ourselves."*
– Lao Tzu, Chinese philosopher

What is leadership? Who is a leader? These questions can be answered in several different ways. Nahavandi (2006) defines leader as "any person who influences individuals and groups within an organization, helps them in the establishment of goals, and guide them toward achievement of these goals, thereby allowing them to be effective" (p. 4). As cited by Aquila (2004), P. F. Drucker believes that "a leader is someone who has followers. Some people are thinkers. Some are prophets. Both roles are important and badly needed. But without followers, there can be no leader" (p. 8). Whichever way you choose to define a leader, one thing does remain: leadership is what differentiates a success organization from a mediocre organization.

Probably very few or any one of us can say we are natural-born leaders. Even fewer of us become effective leaders. Many of us have been exposed to some type of leadership positions. If you have to think back to all the time you have been exposed to different opportunities, how many times have you taken advantage of that opportunity to prove your leadership prowess? True leaders have the ability to sense when there is a leadership vacuum and rise to the occasion.

Leaders such as Mahatma Gandhi, Rev. Martin Luther King Jr., Nelson Mandela, Winston Churchill, and many others, rose on different occasions when leadership was needed. They influenced, captured hearts and minds, and rallied their people to a common cause. Aquila (2004) writes that for anyone to have such impact on others, the leaders need to know who they, need to know what to do, and be role models for other people. What leaders do is find solution to problems, recognize talents, train and develop those talents, empower and delegate, listen with intent to learn, coach and counsel, and motivate and reward excellence. If you are not doing this, you are not a leader by my own definition. Which is *"leadership* is the ability to rally a group of people to a common cause or desired results." Can you become a leader even in the hospitality industry? The answer is yes, because this industry needs leaders, especially in the front lines.

Autocratic Leader
This type of leadership is the old-style leadership. The wants and needs of the employees are second to everything else. Individuals with this type of leadership style make decisions unilaterally without inputs from employees. Giving that not every situation needs employee's input before decision are made, managers should know that the hospitality industry is the peoples industry, not the military where autocratic leadership style is most effective. The hospitality industry is too fluid and in a constant state of flux

to have a rigid leadership style as autocratic. Temperament and patient is needed to handle and deal with people. This leadership style makes the employees dependent on the leader for instructions, directions, and guidelines.

Bureaucratic Leader

The bureaucratic leader makes decision strictly by the book. These types of leaders defer to the company rules and policies for decision making and do not necessarily see any reason to change. For example, two employees report late for work. One reported because he was hitting the snooze button each time the alarm clock goes off; while the other employee is late because of traffic, caused by an accident. A bureaucratic leader may likely reprimand these two employees equally, because the company policy says anyone that comes in late should get a reprimand. With these two instances, the manager should approach the situation differently, as the reasons for coming in late are totally different. After all, company policy is a guide, and leaders should exercise some judicious restrain in their applications.

X and Y Leaders

Douglas McGregor of MIT School of Industrial Management proposed *Theory X* by advancing the notion that organizational assumptions about their employees were wrong and counterproductive. Some manager see employees are lazy and have natural dislike for work, they want to be forced, directed, controlled, or threatened with punishment and lack motivation and not ambitious, will avoid responsibilities, and prefer security over anything else. These types of managers use the autocratic leadership style and are dictatorial. If managers are to see improvement in the performance of their employees, they will have to be more positive and adopt participative management style approach.

McGregor suggested that leaders should put aside this Theory X and espouse what he called *Theory Y*. Theory Y assumes that employees enjoy work and find it to be natural, motivated by the craving to be better, able to exercise self-direction, and solve problem creatively. McGregor believe that whatever assumption a leader has about the employees will determine how the employees are led.

Laissez Faire Leader

These leaders have a-hands-off approach in their leadership styles. They allow employees a lot of latitude in decision making and problem-solving. For this type of leadership style to be effective, the leaders must train, develop, empower and delegate effectively, and ensure that the employees are competent in their judgments. The most important key element in this leadership style is trust. However, this style is least applicable in the hospitality industry.

Democratic Leader

The democratic leader is aware of the people under his leadership. These leaders involve their employees in decision making process. Just as with the autocratic leadership style, not every decision needs employees' input. However, if and when you have made a decision on a particular situation, it may also be important to ask the employees what they think about the situation. If you are convinced that your decision is the right decision, sell the idea to your employees. At the end of it, they may be pleased that you involved them in the decision making process. You may even hear some say, "even though he did not take my idea, I am glad I added my two cents." Make your employees feel special and part of the decision making process by being a democratic leader.

Transactional Leaders

Transactional leaders appeal to the employee self-interest with rewards and incentives. Workers perform their job and are rewarded with pay and rank. This is management by objective because employees perform and complete previously agreed upon tasks. This leadership style does not however use skills as a guide to performance. These leaders seek work for rewards, and do not necessarily build on the employees' necessary skills or do they tap into their creativity. The most effective way to tap into employees' skills and creativity is by transformational leadership style.

Transformational Leaders

With this leadership style, managers get long-term employee commitment to improving performance and job process. Transformational leaders communicate organization vision, mission, and objectives, provide meaningful, challenging, and interesting jobs (Herzberg motivational-hygiene theory), act as coaches, mentors, and developing employees to reach their full potentials (Maslow's hierarchy of needs). By communicating your vision, inspiring your people, and developing them, you are appealing to the employees higher-order needs. This will be beneficial in times of change and difficulty.

Some of the most influential transformational leaders are Mahatma Ghandi, Nelson Mandela, and Dr. Martin Luther King, Jr. These individuals achieved their goals for their people by nonviolence means. In the hospitality industry, people like Walt Disney, Conrad N. Hilton, Norman Brinker, Bill Darden, and Bill Marriott come to mind. One of Wald Disney's famous quotes is:

"You can dream, create, design, and build
the most beautiful place in the world, but
it requires people to make it a reality."
– Walt Disney

This is just one of his famous quotes. He knew fully well that his vision and creative genius alone will not make his theme parks a success without the inclusion of his Cast Members. Another individual with transformational leadership is Horst Schulze. His leadership as Ritz-Carlton's president and chief operating officer lead to the company winning the Malcolm Baldridge National Quality Awards in 1992 and 1999. Making it the first and only hospitality company to win this coveted award two times. A great testimony of transforming Ritz-Carlton to one of the best hospitality companies in the industry.

Situational Leader
The situational model was developed by Kenneth Blanchard and Paul Hersey. The leadership behaviors are classified into two different categories: the directing and supporting styles, and the coaching and delegating styles. The leadership style that is adopted will depend on the situation.

Directing and supporting
Directing style is most used when the leader has an employee that needs to learn the task or job they are suppose to do. The goal is to get the job done. The leader would have to take the employee through every step of the task from the beginning to the completion. This approach is best for new employee training or when teaching a new skill. The **supporting style** is intended for the leader to show some compassion and consideration for their employee by "praising, encouraging, listening to their ideas, involving them in decision making, and helping them reach their own solutions" (Miller, Walker, & Drummond, 2007, p. 50). After employees have settled in their jobs and learned all the tricks, the job is no longer interesting; they are less challenged and motivated, this is the most appropriate time for the leader to move to the second part of the situational leadership.

Coaching and delegating

Coaching style. With the coaching style, the leader continues to use directing style to continue the development of the employee skills, and supporting style to continue to motivate and build on previous commitment by listening more, asking for inputs, and continue involvement in decision making process. As the employees' become more competent and savvy on their jobs, their commitment and passion maybe wavering and uncertain. This is the time to be low on directive and high on supportive. However, when the employee shows high competency and high commitment, the best behavior is ***delegating style***. The delegating style is low on directive and supportive, because this employee has shown some leadership qualities and you should be turning some of your responsibilities to the employee. Delegate some of the operations day-to-day assignments to the employee and provide little direction and support. Using this leadership style helps you to determine committed and competent is the employee, when to intervene, and which assignments to delegate.

Servant Leader

The concept of servant leadership is having the feelings that one really wants to serve; that is serve first and lead second (Bowman, 2003). This theory was first proposed by Robert Greenleaf about forty years ago. Greenleaf belief is that a good leader should:

> ask questions, focus less on productivity and more on voluntary action, employees are colleagues not underlings, is trusting, accepting, open to new ideas, resilient, wise, insightful, imaginative, positive, and possesses a good humor, makes time for people, accepts employees for who they are and not try to re-create them in his image, ask the following question as the ultimate test of good leadership: "do those I serve grow as people?" (p. 261).

In the book of John, chapter 13, Jesus Christ preached, practiced, and demonstrated the concept of servant leadership by washing the feet of his disciples. When it was the turn of Simon Peter, he wanted to know why Jesus Christ was washing his feet. Jesus Christ responded by saying "what I am doing you do not understand now, but you will know after this" (verse 7). They carried on a series of conversations. Finally Jesus Christ said to Simon Peter:

> Do you know what I have done to you? You call Me Teacher and Lord, and you say well, for so I am. 'If I then, your Lord and Teacher, have washed your feet, you also ought to wash one another's feet.' 'For I have given you an example, that you should as I have done to you.' 'Most assuredly, I say to you, a servant is not greater than his master; nor is he who is sent greater than he who sent him.' 'If you know this things, blessed are you if you do them.' 'I do not speak concerning all of you. I know whom I have chosen; but that the Scripture may be fulfilled….. (verses 12-18, p. 726)

As cited in Rowe (2003), Larry Spears, the executive director of Greenleeaf Center for Servant Leadership identified the following 10 skills of servant leader:

1. Listening
2. Empathy
3. Healing
4. Awareness
5. Persuasion
6. Conceptualization
7. Foresight
8. Stewardship
9. Commitment
10. Building community

The servant theory will however be more effectively practiced in a decentralized, bottom-top management decision making process, flatten organizational structure, and an inclusive work environment. In other words, servant leadership is based on the principles of "humility, honesty, trust, empathy, healing, community and service" (Bowman, 2003, p. 257), and managers must see themselves and equal to the employees and work as their "servants or facilitators of their success in the workplace" (Iverson, 2001, pp. 260-261).

> *"Servant leadership is the foundation and the secret of Sam Walton's ability to achieve team synergy."*
> *– Michael Bergdahl*

Primal Leader

Emotional intelligence is a competency every leader should have. Emotional intelligent is the ability to know your environment, your employees, and customers and guests. It is ever essential in this industry if you want to be successful. Through emotional intelligence, the leader is able to know how everyone feels and sense their perspective on issues of importance (Kerfoot, 2004). These leaders identify with their employees and are able to find the unity necessary to build commitment necessary to foster an effective organization. It is the responsibility of leaders to provide assistant to the people that work for them, recognize the employees as equals as well as working harmoniously with their colleagues in a cohesive way, these are leadership models that is needed in every organization.

Through emotional intelligence, the primal leader is able to set the tone and climate that permeates throughout the organization. The role of the primal leader is important in the hospitality industry, because of its level of stress, turnover, people problems, and the need to satisfy guests and meeting the needs of the employees.

Kerfoot (2003) believes that "in your corner people are needed ... to create the positive professional organizations that everyone wants" (p. 358).

10 traits of effective leaders

1. Commitment to success
2. Set proper priorities
3. Set and demand high standards
4. Be tough but fair in dealing with people
5. Concentrates on positives and possibilities
6. Develop and maintain a strong sense of urgency
7. Pay attention to detail
8. Provide for the possibility of failure
9. Be personally involved
10. Have some fun

Knight, C. F., & Dyer, D. (2005). Ten traits of effective leaders, *Harvard Management Update*, 10 (10), 3-6.

The dictionary defines power as ability to control others; authority; influence; and sway. Do you believe in the saying "the end justifies the means?" Are you a hard nose negotiator? Are you manipulative and skillful in persuading others to do things your own way? If you answer yes to any or all of these questions, then you certainly have some of the characteristics of a Machiavellian.

Niccollo Machiavelli (1469-1527), wrote *The Prince.* The concept of The Prince is the ability of any individual to consolidate power by putting self-interest, self-gains, self-importance above the groups and individuals. More so, they are very comfortable using any means at their disposal to achieve personal goals. Leadership without power or influence is like cooking without a recipe. Just as a recipe is necessary to make sure that the meal will turn out right, so is power essential for leaders to get things accomplished. Nahavandi (2006) asserts that without power, leaders will not be effective in guiding their followers to achieve desired goals. Since leaders are expected to do great deeds, it is important then to "provide them wide latitude and power to accomplish their goals" (Nahavandi, 2006, p. 102).

"A leader is one who knows the way,
goes the way, and shows the way."
– John C. Maxwell

Referent Power – people with this type of power influence and attract people with their congenial ways of doing things. People are attracted to them because they are respected, liked, friendly, pleasant, approachable, and pleasing. People with referent power usually have large followers and admirers. Referent power depends on charisma and cachet. As your referent power grows, so does your acceptability, appreciation, identification, and clout. Leaders with referent power find it easier to effectively manage conflicts, deal with marginal employees, and find it easier to persuade others. An individual with this type of power is Michael Jordan. Mr. Jordan contributed billions of dollars to the U.S. economy through basketball and Nike. His face is known worldwide and everyone wants to be like Mike. Well, it does not matter how much Gatorade you drink, you will never be like Mike.

Expert Power – this type of power is based on a person's competence, expertise, knowledge and information in certain area. People comply because they trust the comprehension, aptitude, and the ability of the holder of this power. When you need advice on food preparation and recipe standardization, you go to a chef and not a psychiatrist. When you are ill, you go to a doctor and not an accountant. When you need legal services, you go to a lawyer not psychologist. However, individuals such as doctors, lawyers, professors, psychiatrist, psychologists, and master chefs are examples of expert powers. You start to increase your expert power when you are unbiased and demonstrate that you have nothing to gain personally from influencing and persuading others. However, you start to lose power when you put personal gain and self ahead of everything else.

Legitimate Power – people with this type of power hold formal positions. Their legitimate power is derived from the position they hold. Others comply because they recognize their legitimate position and source of power. Legitimate power usually exists because we believe that people should have this type of power in other to have control and compliance. Among people with this type of power are parents, managers, general managers, presidents, police officers, and teachers.

Reward and Coercive Power – persons with **reward power** have access to rewards and incentives, and use them as a tool to get others to comply. In reward power; they comply because they want the reward. Managers have this power due to their ability to reward their employees with money, special time off, good office view, or a trip. Teachers also have reward power over their students because they have the power to determine if they pass or fail a course. Parents are another example of individuals with reward powers. They can reward with food, candy, sleep-over, television and driving privileges. Individuals with **coercive power** have the ability to punish. They use the source of power to affect people's decision and to comply with orders and instruction. Others comply not necessarily because they agree, but because they fear punishment and possible reprisals from non-compliance. Supervisors have coercive power by reducing employee hours, schedule changes, refusing vacations, and denying days off. As with reward power, teachers have coercive power also. Teachers can offer recommendations and high grades. Teachers can also offer low grades and unfavorable recommendations. Reward power is the opposite of coercive power and individuals with these powers use it as necessary to get people to comply and follow instructions.

Many characteristics distinguish a manager from a leader, and from a leader to a good leader, and from a good leader to an effective leader. This chapter has exposed you to different leadership theories and concepts. Your success as a leader would depend on your abilities to move beyond that management position and into a leadership role. Now are you a manager or a leader? If you still do not know what you are, consider the following.

Real Leaders	Real Managers
• Leaders are original	• Managers copy
• Leaders develop	• Managers maintain
• Leaders are people-focused	• Managers system-focused
• Leaders inspire	• Managers control
• Leaders will ask what and why	• Managers ask how and when
• Leaders make things happen; are thinking about tomorrow, not today; leverage their time to create multiple hours of work for others; and create an environment for success.	• Managers on the other hand like to operate, maintain and upgrade system; they are great storekeepers, and they keep their eyes on the bottom line.

Source: Aquila, A. J., (2004). The eternal riddle of being an effective leader. *Accounting Today*, 8-9.

From this outline, we can conclude that managers do things right, and real leaders do the right things. So, what are you? A leader or you are still a manager? Well, the rest of the chapter will help you determine your actual leadership qualities.

"Organizations endure, however, in proportion to the breadth of the morality by which they are governed. Thus the endurance of organization depends upon the quality of leadership; and that quality derives from the breadth of the morality upon which it rests."
– Chester Irving Barnard

Having read this chapter, you will have to start thinking of your own style of leadership and developing it. The challenge usually is adapting theory to practice. This is what you will have to figure out by yourself because it cannot be taught by anyone but you. Since the theories are different, so also will the practice. Your experience and the situation that you will encounter will determine the leadership style to apply.

Your style of power will be different from your leadership style, as this is an area of expertise. However, referent power can be developed by being a good leader who understands his employees and willing to do anything for them.

Autocratic leader
Bureaucratic leader
Coaching
Coercive power
Delegating
Directing
Democratic leader
Expert power
Laissez Faire leader

Leadership
Legitimate power
Situational leader
Primal leader
Referent power
Reward power
Supporting
Servant leader
Transactional leaders
Transformational leaders
X and Y leaders

Questions and Applications

1. Define the following terms:
    a. Democratic leader
    b. Primal leader
    c. Servant leader
    d. Autocratic leader
    e. Coercive power
    f. Delegating
    g. Coaching
2. How do the terms discussed in this chapter relate to your organization?
3. Which of the leadership concepts discussed in this chapter is applicable within your organization?
4. Which of the leadership styles fits your personality?
5. How would you apply the concept to your location and unit of operation?
6. Why do you think delegation is important?
7. Which of the powers do you believe is more effective?
8. How and when would you use coaching?
9. As a leader, what are some of your obligations to your employee and owner?
10. Why should employees look up to you for leadership?

CHAPTER TWO

Leading by Communicating Effectively

"The strong man is the one who is able to intercept at will the communication between the senses and the mind."
– Napoleon Bonaparte

How important is communication? Do we really need to communicate? The simple answer to these questions in yes! We need to communicate. Every form of behavior, whatever we say, whatever we do, tone of speech or response, facial expressions, choice of words, writings and actions, listening skills; everything we do intentionally or unintentionally sends a message to our listeners. The wish is hopefully the message is communicated effectively and the listener takes the information and uses it as it was intended.

Effective leaders communicate clearly. They have large antenna ears, big eyes, and "walk in others' shoes by listening and caring"

(Alexander, 1997, p. 25). Effective communicators are enriched with good flow of information. Effective communicators use information as a tool to align company goals and vision by sending superior messages. Effective communicators are successful, find pleasure in personal and professional life, have sense of achievement, and form close relationships (Iverson, 2001).

Not every relationship is the same. How is it different? Friendship is different based on individual needs, wants, and convenience. DeVito (2004) asserts that as needs change, so also is the qualities of the friendships. In several instances "old friend are dropped for from the old circles to be replaced by new friends who better serve these new needs" (p. 282). Since the qualities of the friendship changes, so also will the level of relationships and involvements with the new and old friends change.

Overt

This is a type of relationship that is conducted in the open. There is no secrecy and both sides and all sides express desires, thoughts, and feelings overtly. If you like someone, you talk to the person often, whenever you see the person, you laugh, smile, hug, shake hands, express pleasantries, very cheerful and show emotions. You may go further to share personal feelings, family, become family friends, and share family stories. You most often will share your positive attitude with a repeat guest or customer that is easy to please and probably tips very well. On the other hand, if you do not like someone, you let the person know by frowning, ignoring any form of acknowledgement from them, and telling them why we do not like them one way or another. In this form of relationship, you communicate your likes and dislikes one way or another in the open.

Covert

This type of relationship is kept hidden. Your anger, displeasure, or unhappiness is never expressed in the open. Imagine if a guest gets you angry and you tell them how you really feels. You may not have a job moment after you expressed yourself to that guest. Rule of thumb dictates that we check our displeasure and smile at every situation. Furthermore, we are supposed to keep our relationship with others at work hidden. You may to some extent express how you truly feel about a fellow employee. Imagine what would happen if you express how you feel about the knuckle-head manager. Your life or career may be going down-spiral from that moment. With covert relationship, you must be tactful, practice restrain and show no emotions if you want to keep your career on track.

Task

This is the type of relationship you may have with your co-workers. The relationship is strictly about the job. Any time you talk to the employee or your peer, you discuss the job and the job alone. This relationship is far less emotional than overt relationship, where you pretty much wear your pleasure and displeasure on your sleeves. Interactions and information shared are strictly business and business only.

Very few relationships in the place of work are either overt, covert, or task. Majority is a combination of the three. A covert or task relationship breeds room for mistrust and suspicions. An effective leader will want to facilitate an overt relationship, but must be careful and respect any direction the employees chose to go. The hospitality industry most dictates overt relationship because it is people-oriented. Most employees have covert relationships with management because of politicking and uncertainties in the place of work. The leader must be diplomatic and delicate in facilitating an overt relationship in the place of work because an open relationship breeds trust, pleasure, honesty, cooperation and expression of ideas.

Interpersonal communication is one thing we do on a daily basis, but we pay little attention to the effect it has on our lives. We ask questions, talk to coworkers, ask for directions, ask for a date, apply for a job, and talk to our significant other. Just as it is important for the chef to know how reduce or increase recipe, a judge apply the law, a teacher to teach a course, so it is important for you the leader to know the importance of effective communication. Your success to be an effective communicator as a supervisor, a friend, significant other, or a teacher, will largely depend on your interpersonal skills. The following eight skills below, discuss how you could be an effective communicator. As a leader in this industry, you must have dexterity in the way you communicate with your employees and guests. You will not succeed if you send any mixed messages to either party.

Social Intelligence

No leader will be successful without knowing itself, its environment, and its people. Good leaders must know when and how to react to different people and situations. Solving peoples' problem is the duty of a leader, so the leader should know how to respond at the appropriate time. You need to respond to your employees' need appropriately and not alienate them. Appropriate response is not limited to mere showing of concern, but providing proper feedback and follow-up. When employees perform poorly, it is more appropriate to call the employee aside and discuss the performance issue, provide feedback, then coaching on how to turn a poor performer into a star performer.

Technical Competence

Responding correctly to situations that face us tells how effective we are in dealing with everyday issue. Technical competency is the appropriate and correct way to respond to issues. The use of "I" language show that you as the leader is taking responsibility for your words, actions and deeds. You should always start your sentence with "I feel that...," or "I see that....," or "I have noticed lately that ...," or "I believe that..." This style of communication is less judgmental, evaluating, blaming, and accusatory compared to the "You" language. The "You" language is very negative and could put the employee in a defensive mood. Imagine you hearing someone start a sentence by saying "you have not ......" or "you are not always......" or "you do not....." Communication should be positive as much as possible and good leaders should facilitate this as much as possible.

Complete and Specific

Imagine a chef talking to an employee, saying "John, we were busy tonight, and we ran out of chicken breast. Tomorrow, make sure you marinate extra chicken breast to avoid running out." What is wrong with that statement? What if John decides to marinate 100 extra chicken breasts when he may actually need far less than that? The communication is not complete and specific. The leader must be specific to a number, if necessary. To be complete and specific, the leader should specify the amount of chicken breast, and possibly when he wanted the extra prepared, to avoid leftover.

Assertiveness

Assertiveness is the skill needed for delivering your message completely, tactfully, correctly, and succinctly. As a leader, you have the courage to tell the employees how proud you are about their performance. You must also have the same courage when you look at them directly in their eyes and communicate your disappointment to them. However, to be assertive, you must possess social intelligence, because the employees are different and react differently. A good leader will be willing to deliver both good and bad news to their employees on a timely basis. If the employees always hear how good they are doing, and not their challenges, how could they improve poor performance? You will effectively assert yourself if you have social intelligence and are tactful.

Multiple Channels

One of the best ways to communicate effectively is by using multiple channels. Organizations have multiple avenues to communicate company information to their employees. Such channels include the intranet, bulletin boards, company newsletter, memorandums, general meetings and departmental meetings, and one-on-one interactions. By using these channels to communicate, the likelihood of employees missing any company information is minimal. Leaders should take advantage of the resources available to them to communicate with employees as effectively as possible. As a hospitality manager, you are always in the mix of your employees and should talk to them often.

Credibility

Since people follow leaders voluntarily, then the leaders should show integrity every time. It is important for leaders to say what they are going to do, and actually do it. Your credibility is always on the line each time you open your mouth to communicate. You should be congruent in your words and actions. Deliver on promises, do whatever you say you would do, be logical in your convictions, use facts as part of your communication, and model the right image. Your employees are relying on you to lead and guide them; do not disappoint them!

Simplify Language

Speaking a language and using the terms everyone understands is important. Having social intelligence will develop this speaking skill. The hospitality workforce comprises employees from different diverse background such as culture, age, education, language, and experiences. Dealing and working with everyone on the same level could prove to be difficult. However, understanding that differences exists among everyone in the workforce and willing to communicate in a simplified and common language that everyone understands will foster a community with common understanding. You as a leader must find the common ground to reach the employees.

Ask Questions

To seek understanding and ensure that communication is effective, you must ask questions, ans for feedback, and solicit opinions from the employees. As a leader, you want your messages to be, free of ambiguity, and clarified. To achieve this, you should ask probing questions to seek understanding and make sure others understand what you are communicating. The situation may dictate the type of questions; whether it is open-ended, close-ended.

We also listen for different reasons. But most importantly, we listen because we want to hear what others are saying. That being the case, leaders should adjust their listening styles to fit different situations. DeVito (2004) identifies acquisition of knowledge, formation of friendships and love relationships, effect on positive attitudes and behavior of others, knowing when to suspend evaluation, and the ability to assist other people as payoffs of effective listening. Below are eight different listening styles that could assist leaders in adjusting their listening styles in different situations.

Empathy

Before you can really understand what a person means and feels, you have to listen with a higher degree of empathy. Listening with empathy is putting yourself in the speakers position, feel what they are feeling, see things the way they are seeing it, because you have gone through that same experience. To be an effective leader in the hospitality industry, you should listen with empathy. You as the supervisor have probably performed the same job and gone through the same experience the employees you supervise are going through. So, you should be able to empathize with the waiter that complains about a difficult guest, a cook that complains about too many tickets, or a dishwasher that complains about the amount of work to be done. At one time or another, you have probably been in their shoes, and being an empathetic listener is important to show how much you care.

Sympathy

On the other hand, you do not have to have gone through the same experience to know how the employee feels. You already know the nature of the jobs in the hospitality industry. it is only natural to sympathize with any frustration or complains your employees and guests may have.

Show Interest

An effective listener will always show interest in what a speaker is saying. You show interest by making eye contact to show that you are listening, and saying such as "really," "tell me more," "no," "I can't believe that," or "I see." These are called minimal encouragers. Minimal encouragers show that you are interested in what the person is saying. Look at the guests' eyes as they speak to you. That demonstrates that you are listening to their concerns.

Check your Biases

Every one of us has a bias. When listening, it is necessary to set aside that bias and listen with intent to learn and understand what the other has to say. Leaders should not be bias in their listening styles because of the virtue of their position. Checking your biases at the door demonstrates your impartiality and your belief in listening to the employees' needs and wants. The use of your knowledge about the speaker should assist you to understand the underlining message, and avoid letting your bias determine your response.

Reflect Meanings and Feelings

By reflecting meanings and feelings, both the speaker and the receiver are able to determine if the message is being received as intended. You are listening by paying attention to the speaker without offering advice, suggestions, or stating opinions. You are also repeating what the speaker is saying to ensure correctness and understanding. By showing your feelings, you are demonstrating that you know how the speakers feels and you are demonstrating the same feelings. This process allows you to identify some possible information the speaker may be leaving out deliberately or otherwise. This shows the speaker that the listener understands and this leads to better understanding between the two of them.

Ask Questions

The art of questioning leads to good communication. You should ask questions to seek understanding and clarifications. To facilitate this type of listening style, leaders should use open ended questions that will allow the speaker to elaborate more on whatever they are talking about. The use of minimal encouragers will be important here. The line of questioning should be direct, on the topic of discussion, one question at a time, listen after asking the question, and ask a follow-up question for proper understanding.

Paraphrase

Paraphrasing is the process whereby the listener repeats what the speaker is saying in its own words. Paraphrasing is not repeating the statement word for word, but repeating it as much as possible to reflect what the speaker is saying. For example, if the speaker says "I am having a problem with my food and beverage manager," you might repeat the statement by saying "you seem to be having some problems at work with upper management." This provides clarification to both the speaker and listener.

Summarize

Summarizing is the process whereby the speaker and the listener summarize everything that has been discussed to ensure full understanding. Summary statements can help both sides to see communication and their side more clearly. As a leader, it is absolutely important to summarize your discussion with your employees before ending any meeting.

Active Listener

Active listeners are participants in the communication process. They listen with intent to know and understand the subject of discussion. They use minimal encouragers as tools to seek understanding. For example, someone says "the manager rated me as "M" (meet expectations). An active listener may ask a series of open-ended questions to facilitate an understanding between the speaker and the listener. The active listener may ask "why did the manager rate you that way?" "Have you discussed the rating with the manager?" "What are the criteria for rating employee?" The active listener is involved and seeks to know and understand the communication between the two of them.

In-Depth Listener

The in-depth listener is not only an active listener, but taking the information and act on it. In other words, the in-depth listener is looking for the deeper meaning in the message the speaker is conveying. For example, an employee says "my manager is changing my schedule and reducing my hours." The in-depth listener may use minimal encouragers to make the speaker say more, but the more probing questions may follow. Questions such as "why do you think he is doing that" or "do you think he does not like you, and wants you to quit?" Imagine when someone asks you "how do you like my car?" The underline message is the person is asking you to make a positive comment about the car, and not necessarily your true opinion.

Critical and Open-Minded Listener

Effective critical listeners do listen with intent of making a thoughtful assessment or opinion. They listen judiciously and with an open mind. While listening with an open-mind will assist you in understanding the message better, listening critically will help you with analyses and evaluation of the message. In adapting this listening style, you are non-prejudice, you check your biases, keep your feelings out of it, and able to identify fallacies from facts.

Supporting and Non-Critical Listener

The supporting and non-critical listener listens and asks questions to know and understand without being critical of what is being said. Same example as active listener, an employee says his got "M" rating (Meet Expectation) in his performance evaluation; because the manager believes he did not complete some of the projects he was assigned, completed his scheduled trainings, or unable to reduce food costs. As the listener, you should not say he deserves it because his did not do what he was assigned, or the manager was right in his evaluation. You should say something to the effect that now he knows why he got the rating; he should do better next time to avoid the same rating. More so, he now knows where the manager focuses his attention when it comes to rating the employees. He can work to improve these areas. You as the listener reinforce positive behavior to accomplish the goal.

> *"Communication is about being effective,*
> *not always about being proper."*
> *– Bo Bennett*

Passive/Surface Listener

Individuals with this type of listening styles take information as face value. They pay little attention to the details and could make comments carelessly as if they do not care. They see the information being passed on to them as irrelevant and less important. They will probably leave the conversation without gaining anything from it. It is like the popular saying "it goes into one ear, and goes out of the other."

Eye-Avoidance Listener

These individuals listen without looking at the speaker directly in the eyes. They maybe distracted by the surroundings and other barriers to effective listening. However, this type of listening style maybe practiced due to cultural differences. People of Asian descent, especially the Japanese will often listen without making direct eye contact. This should not be considered to be a sign of ineffective listening because; it is considered as a sign of disrespect to make direct eye contact for a longer period of time.

Thought-Completing Listener

Every one of us is almost guilty of this listening style. The idea to complete someone's sentence is so common that we do not often complete them correctly. Imagine a guest in the hotel saying "excuse me... I am looking for the...." And the employees said "the bathroom?" And, the guest says "no, the front desk." As a leader, wait patiently and let the employee finish speaking before responding. This shows that you were listening and not thinking about a response while the speaker is still speaking.

Pre-Occupied Listeners

These listeners have other things on their mind while listening. They are not paying complete attention to the speaker and their mind is focused on something else. I had a student in one of my classes who requested to have his cell phone on because his wife was due at any moment. I agreed, as it was a joyful moment to be awaiting his new son. I called on him twice in the class, he did not respond. Someone had to touch him, before he could respond, because his mind was with his wife, but his body in the classroom. However, when his cell phone rang, he picked it up as fast as lighting.

Insulated Listeners

These listeners have some amount of the information the speaker is delivering. They listen to the speaker because they are required to or have to. However, they leave with the same amount of information they came in with. Literarily speaking, whatever you say enters one ear and goes out through the other. Employees that are angry when you call them into your office will most likely be insulated listeners because that anger will block anything you have to say. The best time is to wait and have a cooling period.

Selective Listeners

These listeners pick and choose what they want to hear. In most instances, the information they take away are information they can use and of benefit to them. Every other information is irrelevant, and they do not care to hear it. As a leader, you cannot pick and choose what you hear from your employees. Information is relevant; listen to it.

Defensive listeners

These types of listeners have one thing on their mind: they are listening to the speaker to defend themselves. Whatever you say is considered an attack on them and their actions. They come to listen with their minds made up and are ready to defend themselves against what they consider an attack on them. If you always tell employees what they do wrong, they will become defensive listeners each time you call them to your office.

Ambush Listeners

This type of listener waits to see contradiction in your speech and leaps to point it out to you. Sometimes, the comment may not necessary be contradictory, but the perception of the listener makes it so. This listener leaps to point it out and makes sure you hear what he has to say about it. As a leader, you must be ready to accept any form of criticism without taking it personal. After all, that is what separates you from the rest.

"Walt put everything he knew about communication with images into the park, so it was very familiar."
– John Hench

Relationships are nurtured by good communication. As a leader, nothing is more important to you than communicating with the employees by listening to them. Your ability to relate to them in times of need will determine whether they will trust you or not. It is most likely that you have done most of the jobs in the hospitality industry. So it is important and necessary that you relate to them by empathizing when the time arises. If you have not experience the job that they are performing, try to sympathize with them by putting yourself in their shoes. Your style of communication, relationship, listening, and interaction should be determined by the people that surrounds you, the guests, and situation.

Active Listener
Ask Questions
Assertiveness
Check your Biases
Complete and Specific
Covert
Credibility
Critical and Open-Minded Listener
Empathy/Sympathy
Eye-Avoidance Listener
In-Depth Listener
Insulated Listener
Multiple Channels
Overt
Paraphrase
Passive/Surface Listener
Pre-Occupied Listener
Reflect Meanings and Feelings
Selective Listener

Show Interest
Simplify Language
Social Intelligence
Summarize
Supporting and Non-Critical Listener
Task
Technical Competence
Thought-Completing Listener

Questions and Applications

1. Define the following concepts:
   a. Covert relationship
   b. Multiple channels
   c. Simplify language
   d. Selective listener
   e. Critical and Open-Minded Listener
   f. Thought-completing listener
   g. Technical competent
2. Explain how social intelligence can help you as a supervisor
3. How would reflecting meanings and feelings help you to understand the employees more effectively?
4. How can checking your biases help you with open communication?
5. Why do you think empathy and sympathy are important to you? How would you apply them within your operations?
6. How important is effective listening to you?

CHAPTER THREE

Leadership and Motivation

"Motivation is the art of getting people to do what you want them to do because they want to do it."
– Dwight D. Eisenhower

When you decide to lose weight, what is it that you need to do? You eat with moderation, eat food with less fat and calories, eat healthy, eat early in the evening instead of bedtime, and exercise more frequently. Ask those struggling with their weight and on diet, they will probably tell you that they follow the entire weight lose rule. Give them all the benefit of the doubt until you see them on a buffet line. You will be at awe. The same rules apply in the place of work in regards to motivation. When all the rules are followed, employee morale will improve, when we break the rule, morale suffer, employees feel dissatisfied, and complacency sets in.

At all levels of an organization employees want to be respected, appreciated, and motivated. Gone are the days where we look up to the managers and human resources for motivation. Building a motivating workplace environment is the responsibility of everyone in the workforce. Choosing the right tools and time is the key to successful motivation.

Motivating and Energizing Your Team: 10 Tips for Success

1. Affirm the presence of all your teammates by greeting and acknowledging them every day.

2. Affirm teammates' concern questions, and issues with consistent follow-up and follow-through.

3. Affirm the competent performance of routine tasks by recognizing and appreciating them.

4. Affirm any and all "extra efforts" by recognizing appreciating them.

5. Affirm your teammates' development by providing on performance.

6. Affirm the competency of your teammates by assigning them special responsibilities, roles, or projects.

7. Affirm your teammates' role by sharing/explaining "big picture" information.

8. Affirm your teammates' potential by making suitable training/development opportunities available.

9. Affirm the competency of your teammates by seeking their input and involvement in solving problems/facing challenges.

10. Affirm the contributions of your teammates by celebrating and publicizing their achievement.

Source: William A. Marzano (2005). Motivating and energizing your team: 10 tips for success, *Academic Leader*, 21 (5), 4-5.

Motivation is the factor that drives us to do what we do everyday. It is that fire that burns in us that makes us wake up early in the morning and make it to work or school, take chances even though we cannot predict the outcome, and take risk to fulfill our satisfaction. Whether you believe it or not, everyone has a theory on how to motivate people. Several theories maybe familiar to you, others may not. Below are some motivational theories.

A well-known psychologist Abraham Maslow, developed a theory he called *Hierarchy of Needs*. At the nucleus of Maslow's theory are human needs. Maslow believes that much of what we do is based on meeting unfulfilled human needs and wants which are both physiological and physical (Iverson, 2001; Tesone, 2005). Humans, he said are animal wanting. They will behave in a way that will satisfy their needs and wants. He believes that we are motivated by higher needs as we meet lower level needs. He theorized five levels of needs.

At the bottom of the hierarchy are *physiological needs*. These are things human need for survival. These needs are food, water, air, shelter, sex. When these needs are not met, we channel every effort we have towards fulfilling them. Imagine an employee that has not eaten. Can such an individual think straight? All he has on his mind is food, and when he can take a break and refuel his stomach. When these needs are met, we move on to a higher need. The next level of need is *safety needs*. These needs are structure, stability, order and security, liberty from terror, worry, and turmoil. For the hospitality employees, this may be the different between committing themselves to the job and moving from job to job. Though, there is no such thing as "*job security*," having the awareness that there is no fear of losing your job is part of meeting the safety needs. As these needs are fulfilled, the next is *social needs*. These needs include being accepted, to belong, to be liked, love and be loved. To the hospitality employee, social needs are very important as the industry is *"peoples' industry."* socialization in the place of work is as important as anything else. We spend an average of six hours a day and 30 hours a week with other employees; and sometimes, more than we spend with our own family. Being accepted fulfills this need, which then leads to **esteem needs**. This need is sometime referred to as ego needs. This is the desire for self-respect, self-esteem, recognition, praise, attention, appreciation, and dignity. Praising, rewarding, and recognizing good performances are good ways to motivate and improve self-worth. It is even more important if the praise and reward is given at an appropriate time and place. The last and at the top of the hierarchy is the need for **self-actualization**. This is the need to be doing what one does best, desire career, challenging work, and achieving success and become all you can become in a holistic sense; you are content, at peace, having attained self-perceived level of spiritual and self-content (Tesone, 2005).

To have the maximum impact expected, you should match rewards with employee needs. Employee that desire time-off to be with family and friends is seeking social need. Giving the employee food will not meet the employee needs.

Practical application

Physiological Needs	Provide employees with regular breaks, employee meals (free if possible or affordable price), employee cafeteria, and locker rooms for convenience, uniforms and laundry benefits.
Safety Needs	Provide a safe working environment by having a well lighted and open parking lot, non-skid shoes, and non-slid floor mats, good and up-to-date equipments with proper training on how to use them, and fire extinguishers.

Social Needs	You should provide the employees with other opportunities to interact with their coworkers outside the regularly scheduled work hours. Opportunities such as holiday parties, after work activities, picnics, or other opportunities will meet social needs.
Esteem Needs	Stroking our ego is one thing that motivates, reassure, and restore our self-esteem. Provide recognition programs such as employee of the month, or quarter, or year; opportunities for promotions, and share guest/customer comment cards.
Self-Actualization	Every employee wants self-satisfaction by achieving their goals. Provide the employees good training and development opportunities, career management opportunities, and/or tuition assistance/reimbursement.

Another psychologist Frederick Herzberg, explained that human relations alone cannot motivate employee performance. He identified several factors that he believes are true motivators. Herzberg found that factors such as company policy, schedules, wages and salaries, compensation, working conditions, the supervisors, and many more do create discontent and dissatisfaction on the job if they are inadequate. These he considers *dissatisfiers*.

However, the removal of anything that causes dissatisfaction does not necessarily motivate either. These Herzberg called hygiene factors; they are also commonly called *maintenance factors*. For example, if you think your supervisor is incompetent, company policy is very rigid, and you are underpaid; all these can lead to tardiness, absenteeism, and poor performance. Changing the supervisor or increasing the pay will not make the employee work harder as soon as the excitement is no longer there. In contrast, Herzberg believed that factors such as employee recognition, meaning responsibility, achievement, growth opportunities, and positive work environment do provide both motivation and job satisfaction. These he called **motivators**. For example, if you get employees involve in decision making, allow the employees to show their creativity and applaud them for their work and efforts, you will see motivation at work. In other words, motivating employees is totally connected to the job according to Herzberg.

Herzberg's theory also consists of two types of reward. The first one is called **intrinsic reward.** Intrinsic rewards are those that are within the control of the individual. These are usually internal and are derived from the job itself. The employee does not depend on anyone for this reward. It is a personal feeling of competency, accomplishment, and personal development gained from doing the work. It is having the feeling that you have done something very good and feels proud of your work (feeling like a million dollars). The other reward is **extrinsic rewards.** These rewards are totally out of the control of the individuals. They are usually given by someone else like the manager, guests/customers, or the organization. Extrinsic rewards alone are not motivation; they can either lead to satisfaction or dissatisfaction. The only true motivators are intrinsic rewards, even though they only affect us when we derive satisfaction from the work environment.

Herzberg motivational-hygiene theory can be beneficial if management recognized that good pay, benefits, and work conditions are motivators. But, these alone may not be enough to completely motivate employees to perform at their best. Provide employees with challenging work and give them some control over their work and create that environment where they can take ownership of their work. Some higher achievers may need additional and challenging responsibilities to be intrinsically motivated. Also, assign employees work they particularly enjoy and like to do.

Follow the 10 Commandment of Employee Motivation

Build self-respect: Positive reinforcement allows people to understand that their efforts add value to the organization.	Don't be neurotic (or disguise it well): Employees deserve to have a clear understanding of what behavior and outcome are expected.
Show respect: Managers often treat employees like a child in an adult-like relationship. An adult-like transaction requires that we allow employees the latitude to solve problems.	Live integrity: In the Dr. Suess book "Horton Hatches the Egg," Horton the elephant gives his word to a lazy bird named Mayzie that she will sit on her eggs until she comes back. Mayzie did not come back and Horton preserves through the ice storms hunters and even a trip to the zoo.
Be fair: In a world where there isn't much that is fair, we need to find ways to be as fair as possible.	Value and reinforce ideas: According to an Employee Involvement Association study, the average employee in Japan submits 32 ideas for improvement per year, compared with 0.17 for the average employee in the United States. That is a ratio of 188-1.

Give them what they want: My mother loves craft. I love books. Every year for Christmas, my mother has given me crafts. I give my mother books. What is wrong with this picture? We love to give what we actually love to receive, so sometimes we forget whom we are doing it for. Each of your employees has a difference preference in rewards.	Give immediate feedback: Whoever created the yearly performance review anyway? By itself, there is really nothing wrong with it, but somewhere along the path, we assume that all feedback get stuck in a file and delivered yearly.
Reinforce the right things: One of the companies I have done work for believed that good employees come to work early and stay late. Not surprisingly, the CEO comes to work early and stayed late. When a new CEO came, he placed emphasis on performance, and productivity went up miraculously.	Serve others: We've all seen it in our mission statement. "To be a leading provider of blah, blah services in our service area providing quality service and a good return to our stakeholders." Gag me with a shovel! To say we are in business to profit is like saying we are alive to breathe.

Source: Roxanne Emmerich, (2005). Follow the 10 commandments of employee motivation. *Des Moine Business Record*, 23 (20), 26-27.

According to David McClelland, humans develop needs according to life experience. Our experiences both in life and at work determine our drive to satisfy our needs. McClelland believes that these needs are: power, affiliation, and achievement.

Employees driven by the ***need for power*** have the tendency to control, manipulate, and exert influence on people's behavior and events. McClelland also identifies two forms of need for power: the need for personal power, or the aspiration to manipulate, control and influence others. The second is the need for social power, or the need to wield authority more conscientiously to achieve set organizational goals and objectives for the common good of all (Iverson, 2001). Those that yearn for the **need for affiliation** want to be part of something. They want friends, meaningful associations, and good relationships with their fellow workers, and clients. These individuals volunteer for activities and committees because they want to be known as part of the process. Those with the **need for achievement** are driven by the will to do something challenging, difficult, master multifaceted tasks and solve complex problems. If you observe the workplace closely, you will notice that these individuals with need for affiliations are surrounded by pictures of the family, plaques, certificates, diplomas, and trophies (Tesone, 2005). All these artifacts are as result of their achievements. This could be refereed to as nonverbal power.

McClelland believes that individuals with high need for personal achievement, joined with high need for social power are the best managers and leaders. Individuals with high needs for affiliations may have supervision of their employees to be a challenge because of their need to have affiliation with people. The supervisor with this need may be nice and close with the employees. However, there will be times when the leader will have to make a decision; the affiliations with their employees may cloud their judgments.

Need for Power	Individuals with high need for power are always seeking leadership position within the workplace. They want to take leadership roles in other to satisfy these needs. Your job as a leader is to steer these individuals to the right directions, such as chairs of committees, writing new training manuals, or mentors to new and dependent employees.

Need for Affiliation	These individuals want to be a part of a group, or affiliated with something. They want meaningful relationships with their coworkers and clients. Being accepted is paramount to these individuals. As a leader, assign them to lead or be a part of the picnic committee, holiday celebrations, conduct customer surveys, or community relations.
Need for Achievement	These individuals are highly interested in continue learning and developing their skills. Achieving their career is more important than anything else. As a leader, provide these individuals with any meaningful assignment that provide some challenges. Tasks such as menu engineering, writing training manuals, enhancing previous communication process or developing new avenues, and developing new guest contacts.

Depending of whom you ask, money may be a motivator or a dis-satisfier. This may be due to the fact that issues of wages and salaries are out of the employees' control, because we are all paid for time worked. When we get a merit raise, we are content and happy. After a while, it becomes expected because it is a reward for the work we perform. It then becomes something we expect and not necessarily a huge motivational factor. Money, being a scarce commodity, employers have to budget this resource to meet every need without running out of this essential commodity necessary to keep the organization afloat.

*"If money was my only motivation, I
would organize myself differently."*
Placido Domingo

According to the equity theory, we develop some beliefs of what we believe we are worth and expectations of what we should be paid. Then, we compare our pay and rewords to others to determine whether there is inequity. If we are able to determine that there is inequity, we develop conflict that motivates us to decrease our production output: this is ***negative inequity***. However, if we are able to determine that we are compensated more than others, we work harder and find way to increase our production output: this is ***positive inequity***.

How do you think your employees would react when they feel they are underpaid? There is no way you can predict the employees' course of action. However, research has indicated that employees would consistently work less to compensate for the reward not provided. This theory believes that employee will choose a course of action that is least costly to them. Employees that feel overpaid, which is very rare to imagine, would increase their productivity and quality of their work to make-up for the over compensations.

Know that equity theory is important. Even more important is the consequences of rewarding some employees and neglecting others. As a leader, rewards should be given out on a timely basis, and a fairly rewarded employee will increase its productivity. Pay your employees better wages and have better incentives than your competitions. A motivated but poorly paid employee will be lured by the competition. Furthermore, do not continuously single out one employee, and compare other employees to this employee. This practice may not be motivating to others. It may backfire if other employees feel that they are less deserving of that employee that gets the accolades all the time.

Edwin Locke developed the goal setting theory. He believed that effective goal setting will result in high motivation because the goal has to be accomplished. A *goal* is a level of performance, accomplishment, or a stage an individual aspires to. It is our goal that directs our behavior that motivates and energizes us to work harder and behave the way we do.

However, to get the most out of goal setting, the following must be considered:

Goal must be specific. Making goals specific is an effective way of knowing what we are aspiring for. If the goal is vague, it is left to the interpretation of anyone. Setting a goal to reduce labor cost is a goal, but it is not specific. If you set the goal to reduce labor cost by 20 percent, you are setting a specific goal. No one can misinterpret this goal because it is clear and specific.

Goal must be acceptable. It is a good intention on the part of the manager to set goals for the employees. It is even a better intention if the employees are consulted in the goal setting. Every one of us work hard to achieve our desire goals, employees should be involved in decisions that affect them. One of these decisions is goal setting. Setting a goal for an employee to improve performance is a good goal setting, but you should know from the employee stand point if they can accept this goal.

Goal must be challenging. By accepting the goal for improving performance, the employee must see some challenges in it or else it will defeat the purpose. By making the goal challenging and accomplishing it, the employee will learn new skills in the process, and will set their eye sights on further higher goals.

Goal must be measurable. The goal must be measurable for the purpose of formative evaluations. Make room for feedback and have checkpoints at intervals to see how the employee is doing. If the employee is doing very well, you may make the goal a little more challenging. If the employee is not doing well, change the goal as the employee continues and adjusts accordingly from there.

Goal setting should move beyond yearly appraisal and merit increment. Leaders should set goals with employees' participations; meet frequently to measure progress, adjust goals as necessary, and celebrate small gains with an eye towards the big prize. Leaders should set goals with new employees to acquire the skills necessary to accomplish their new tasks and positions, while goals for seasoned employees should be geared towards their career ambition and assist them in upward mobility. One of the keys is to always celebrate employee successes.

According to the reinforcement theory, the behaviors that humans continuously engage in are determined by the result we receive from them: this is the *law of effect*. The law of effect states that "behavior that result in a pleasant outcome is likely to be repeated, whereas behavior that results in an unpleasant outcome is not likely to be repeated" (Iverson, 2001). This theory assumes that we are stimulated to repeat our actions by external feedback we receive.

This theory was developed by B. F. Skinner. This theory is of the conviction that our behavior is managed by influencing its outcome. If we are rewarded for a behavior, the number of times we are engaged in that behavior will increase. Also, if we are not punished or ignored for undesirable behavior, the number of times this behavior occurs will increase. However, Skinner highly advocates rewards or positive reinforcement. As cited by Iverson (2001), Luthans and Kreitner outline the following five modification behaviors for improving employees' performance that are beneficial to the organization:

Identify critical behavior. These are the behaviors that the employees must demonstrate to achieve performance improvement.

Set the base line. The base line is the average rate these behaviors should occur.

Determine triggering conditions. You should identify reasons that encourage desired behavior and reasons that hinder those behaviors also.

Create an intervention. Having identified the reasons that promote desired behavior and those that hinder them, put in place a reward system that encourage the desired behavior and consequences for exhibiting undesired behavior.

Evaluate. At this point, you need to do a summative evaluation to compare the base line rate of recurrence of the critical behavior at the beginning with the base line rate of recurrence of the critical behavior the end. You will be able to determine any improvement by doing this. It is also important to have everything written down for possible formative evaluation.

Positive reinforcement is a good and powerful tool to use in gaining employees' commitment, loyalty, and support. It should be used more frequently to improve employee performance by giving meaningful rewards, praise, and recognition. Negative reinforcement or punishment should be used to the barest minimum except it is absolutely necessary. The use of punishment by leaders can severely hinder management-employees relationships. This can lead to disloyalty, apathy, lack of motivation, and disengagement.

"The greater the loyalty of a group toward the group, the greater is the motivation among the members to achieve the goals of the group, and the greater the probability that the group will achieve its goals."
– Rensis Likert

Motivation is such a big factor in getting employees' loyalty. You will lead a successful, dedicated, and loyal team if you know how to motivate the employees. However, you must know what motivates the individual employee to be successful. The general believe that money is a true motivator is false, because not every employee needs money to be motivated. Knowing the motivational theories is important, but applying the theories properly is even more important.

Behavior modification
Dissatisfiers
Economic Man Theory
Equity Theory
Esteem needs
Evaluate
Extrinsic rewards
Goal
Goal Setting
Herzberg Motivational Hygiene Theory
Identify critical behavior
Intrinsic reward
Law of effect
Maintenance factors
Maslow's Hierarchy of Needs
Mcclellan's Theory
Motivators
Need for achievement
Need for affiliation
Need for power
Negative inequity
Physiological needs
Positive inequity
Reinforcement Theory
Safety needs
Self-actualization
Social needs

1. As a manager, what are some of your expectations and needs?
2. What do you think employees expect from you as a form of motivation?
3. Do you believe employees and managers have the same motivations? Why or why not?
4. Which of the followings would you consider employees' needs, and which are managers' needs?
   a. Upward mobility
   b. Appreciation
   c. Learning new skills
   d. Good salaries and wages
   e. Job security
   f. Positive work environment
   g. Adherence to company policies
   h. Good on the job training
   i. Good supervision
   j. Saying thank you
5. Which motivational theory do you believe is most effective? Why do you believe so?
6. What are the differences between Maslow's self-actualization and Mcclellan's theories of motivation?
7. Why do you think motivation is important in the hospitality industry?
8. Why do you think employees' lose their motivation?
9. Would you use the same motivation techniques for the front and back of the house employees? Why?
10. What do you believe is the most important aspect of goal setting?
11. Write your goal for the next five years with a time line for achieving it.

CHAPTER FOUR

Leading by Training and Development

"Training is all-encompassing and should be related to everything a unit does, or can have happen to it."
– Arthur Collins

In the hospitality industry, any company that does not train its employees is doomed to have problems and challenges with productivity and their guests/customers. The necessary skills and knowledge needed to do the job must be attained by the employees if they are to be successful. To narrow the knowledge gap, and maintain competitive advantage, organizations must invest a lot of money on training its employees to acquire the necessary skills and know how of performing the job. In most cases, new employees are usually paired with designated departmental trainers, who would train them on the skills necessary to perform their new responsibility.

In The Beginning: Orientation. Training should always begin with the basics. That is organizational history, culture, rules, policies and procedures. This is the orientation of new employees coming into the organization – ***acculturation***; and the continuous training of those already within the system – ***enculturation***.

Iverson (2001) believes that any orientation should include the following:
- Description of the organization, its history, mission, and function.
- Company policies, rules, and regulations include dress code.
- Compensation and benefits.
- Work schedule and departmental rules.
- Safety procedures.
- Tour of the operation and introduction to key employees
- Introduction to the work group.

After orientation, it is time to train the employee. JIT component is step-by-step teaching of the job – sometime called on-the-job training. To begin this process, all the training steps necessary to complete the training successfully should be outlined. Then, list all the key points the employee must need to effectively complete the performance of the job. Every training method that would assist in the training of the employee should be utilized. It maybe necessary to do a ***pre-test*** to determine the experience and skill of the employee before the training begins. This will determine whether the training will be a few days, or weeks, or months.

Training consists of the following five stages:

Stage 1:   *Prepare the training.* As you are set to begin the training, review the objectives, address any concerns, discuss the hours, location, and methods. Your goal at this stage is put the trainee at ease and motivated.

Stage 2:   *Demonstrate the task or skill* (what the trainee must learn). This is the show and tell stage. You show what the employee needs to know, tell the employee what he needs to know, and show the employee what he needs to know, again.

Stage 3:   *The trainee performs the task.* As the trainee performs that task, the trainer looks on for any possible corrections. The trainee should perform the task repeatedly until the performance is satisfactory.

Step 4:   *Feedback and follow-up.* At this stage, you provide the employee feedback on the performance. On the areas that the trainee needs improvement, set a goal, and a date for further follow up.

Stage 5:   *It is show time.* The employee is now ready to perform the tasks with limited supervision until mastery is achieved. The employee should be under the supervision of a mentor that will further develop the trainee on other aspects of the job function.

Don't train employees in a silo: Think "outside the classroom" for better results.

Eight keys to more efficient and productive training:

- Don't get preoccupied with seating arrangements and AV equipments.
- Training modules or programs must be consistent and compatible with each other.
- Training always takes place in the broader organizational context and culture.
- Get inter-personal
- Leading sets the tone.
- Prepare your folks before "sending them out for training."
- Actively support learning when employees get back home.

- Assess training impact directly on targeted behaviors and organizational performance.

Source: John Kello, (2005). Don't train employees in a silo: Think "outside the classroom" for better results.

Training Content

As you consider designing the training content, you must include the performance standard, analyze the job in its entirety, analyze every component that consist the unit of the job, and all the tasks that comprise each unit. Now, you must decide how you want each unit of the job to be performed, and to the standard you want it. At this point, you should develop and detail the performance of the job from beginning to the end. This will show the trainer and trainee the step-by-step stages of the entire training process.

Training Units

The training unit is the nuts and bolts of the training process. It is the *why*: the reason for the training and how much time will be dedicated to each unit of the task; *how*: the way the training is going to be conducted; *when*: the best, most convenient and appropriate time the training should start and end; *where*: the location the training should be conducted; *what*: this comprises all the things (materials) you need to successfully conduct the training. These are training manuals, pens, papers, games, etc.

Training Implementation

Now you are ready to perform the training. During JIT, you performed a pretest to determine the new employee's knowledge. That information may be useful at this point as you determine how much training and time will be necessary. As the task is performed, the trainee watches; then the trainee performs the task to ensure understanding. This process maybe repeated as often as necessary until the trainee shows an understanding and can perform the task with little or no supervision..

Continuous Improvement

When the training is complete, seek feedback from both the trainer and trainee. From the trainer, you may want to know if the employee learns as much as possible to begin performing the task with limited supervision; the areas the employee shows great interest and improvement; which areas need further training; and overall assessment of the training process. On the part of the trainee, you may want to know if they are comfortable to begin the performance of their job with limited supervision; their areas of strength and further development; their opinion of the training and the entire training process. These questions will give you insight on which areas need changing and which areas need improvement. This is important because employees perform training majority of the time. So, getting their opinions is a valuable tool in the process of improving the training program.

Formative Evaluation

Formative evaluation is the process you will use to determine if the training is progressing as expected. You find this out by observation, interviews, formal and informal surveys, monitoring, and having both formal and informal conversation while the training is going on. Formative evaluation is good at recognizing any faults that exist and make corrections in a real time basis.

Summative Evaluation

Summative evaluation is what you do at the end of the training. This measures the success or failure of the training. Summative evaluation could be looked at by asking the following questions:

Response: Did the employee reaction during and after the training positive or negative? And how much did the employee like the training?

Conduct: Is the employee behavior different after the training? Is the employee using the newly acquired skills on the job?

Mind-set: What is the attitude of the employee? Is the employee demonstrating any new attitude on the job?

Information: Did the employee learn anything new from the training? Did the employee gain any knowledge from the information provided?

Efficiency: As a result of the training, is the employee productivity increasing? Is the training money and time well-spent?

Benefits of Training

Just as it is important to delegate some of your responsibilities to your employees, it is also important that you provide quality training to your employees. The training is performed with the same standard and procedure without reinvention by different trainers. Every employee will learn the same content, information, performance standard, and the goals and objectives are clear.

Benefits to you the supervisor includes:

- Gives you more time to manage and coach.
- You will lead a group of knowledgeable individuals who have been trained using the same standard procedures.
- You will have happier repeat guests and customers.
- All the employees will know what is expected from each other. If an employee is absent, any employee can perform that task with the same standard and procedure and still maintain good service and product.
- It reduces employee turnover and absenteeism because they know what is expected from them.
- The training will reduce your costs as every employee knows the proper measurements and procedures for spoilage, spills, and wastes.
- Good training can help you further your career.

On the side of the employees, training benefits them the following ways:

- Training can improve employee motivation, morale, job satisfaction, and job enrichment.
- Training will increase their knowledge base and will not always ask you what, how, where, when, who about the job.
- Employee tensions will be reduced as everyone knows the expectations of the job.
- Training increases safety and quality of foods and service; reduces accidents and injuries.
- Training can give employees opportunity to grow within the company.

Challenges with Training

In our industry, managers do not train for several reasons. They are putting out fire and doing several things at the same time. These are some of the reason managers give for not providing training:

- I need someone fast and now. The industry is always in a state of flux and the manager needs to fill a position fast.
- There is constant turnover. Managers may not want to train if they know the employee will only stay for a short period of time.
- Managers are too busy to make time for these trainings. This process produces mediocre employees at their best.
- A significant number of the employees in the industry are part time.
- The diversity of the employees could be challenging. A group of new trainees could comprise of employees from different culture, education, varying experiences and knowledge, and age.

Radisson training Initiative

RADISSON SAS Hotels & Resorts is to give 1,500 of its employees specialized training. Staff will be trained to achieve the MPI's (Meeting Professional International) Certificate in Meeting Management (CMM).

The initiative has been undertaken because Radisson's research has shown that meetings planners value service above hi-tech facilities.

"Our strategic partnership with MPI and the CMM designation will add a whole new dimension to our investment in education of our employees," said Marcus Bernhardt, senior vice president and chief operating officer at Radisson. "As a result, the meeting intelligence at Radisson SAS will significantly benefit our meeting planner clients, and our know-how will ultimately bring the meeting experiences to a new level for our guests."

Source: (2003) Radisson training initiative. *Business Travel World*, 34.

"The good news is that the brain is plastic throughout life
- it is shaped through repeated training and experience."
– Daniel Goleman

How could you be successful if you refuse to train and develop your employees? Many managers do not train for several reasons. Some of the reasons I have heard are time constraint, most employees are part time, no training necessary because the skill levels required to perform some of the work are not high, training budget is low, and if I train they will leave for a better job. Irrespective of your reason for not training, remember that you want employees with knowledge for the work they perform. Lack of training can result in frustration, aggravation, irritation, and exasperation. A good and effective leader would equipped her employees with everything necessary to do their work, this include good training. You want knowledge based employees; this is what separates you from your competition. No guest wants to enter your property and get mediocre service or product. If you want happy and repeat guest, and equally happy and motivated employees, train your workers.

Acculturation
Benefits of Training
Challenges with Training
Continuous improvement
Enculturation
Formative evaluation
Job instruction training (JIT)
Orientation
Pre-test
Summative evaluation
Training content
Training for return on investment (ROI)
Training implementation
Training units

1. Why do you think training is very important in this industry?
2. How would you incorporate transformational leadership and training?
3. Why do you think formative and summative evaluations are important?
4. What are some of the ways to ensure consistencies in training?
5. Which training method do you believe is the most effective? Why?
6. What is return on investment (ROI)? Why is it important?
7. What are the benefits of using a pre-test before training?
8. Why do you think supervisors seldom conduct training?
9. How do you think employees learn best in this industry?
10. Who is more logical to conduct training? Why?

CHAPTER FIVE

Leading Through Empowerment and Delegation

"The best executive is one who has sense enough to pick good people to do what he wants done, and self-restraint enough to keep from meddling with them while they do it."
– Theodore Roosevelt

Leading by Empowering

What is wrong with letting employees make decisions within their job responsibilities? What is wrong with teaching your employees how to do your job? What is wrong with letting the employees do your job? What is wrong with you getting paid, while others perform your duties? The answer to these questions is "absolutely nothing." Empowering employees could be one of the most powerful tools to develop employees, motivate them to perform at a higher output, and provide them a sense of accomplishment. An effective leader must know how to empower and delegate responsibilities. The tools to empowerment according to Nahavandi (2006) are "giving employees control over how they perform their work and over their work environment and building a sense of self-efficacy or competence by providing them the opportunities to succeed" (p. 120). Furthermore, creating a participative environment where goal setting, mentoring, coaching, and performance is often rewarded will make empowerment an effective tool for leaders and organizations.

The hospitality is an industry that empowerment and delegation can really be practiced because of the needs of the guests and customers. Managers are often too busy putting out fires and solving minor problems that employees could be attending to. This will free up the managers time to do more important things.

Before delegation can be effective, we must first identify and discuss dimensions of delegation. The following four steps are necessary for delegation to be effectively carried out.

Employee
Before you delegate, you must assess the skills of the delegate (employee). The employee should have the minimum competency to get the job done to an acceptable level. Remember, the employee is doing your work for you, so you must be careful whom you pick to perform this task.

Responsibility
Responsibility is the task you want the employee to perform for you. You have to choose this responsibility carefully, also with the capability of the employee in mind.

Authority
Once you have delegated the responsibility, you must ask yourself: did I give enough authority to this employee to get the job done? If you did not, then you have not delegated effectively. Knowing that

the employee is doing one of your tasks as a manager, it is essential for the employee to be given full authority if the task is to be accomplished successfully. Robbins and Hunsaker (2006) further ask "did I give my subordinate enough authority to get the materials, the use of equipment, and the support from others necessary to the job done?" (p. 136). If the answers to this questions are no, then you cannot hold the employee accountable. Without the authority to do the job, the employee would fail as the employee's peers would simply ignore the employee.

Accountability

After identifying the employee, you have assigned the responsibility, and given the authority to carry out the responsibility, now comes the time to hold the person accountable. For the delegation to be complete there must be some accountability on the part of the employee. Accountability means that the employee is under an agreement to produce the result the manager expects. However, delegating does not in anyway relieve you the leader of the responsibility. The ultimate accountability still rests on you to make sure the job is completed successfully.

Once you has decided to follow-up with empowerment initiative as part of your leadership philosophy, you must consider culture of your organization and the employees you are about to give this new power. Consider the following characteristics before you do anything.

Prudence

Do the employees have the sense that the power about to be given by the manager will help enhance the performance of their jobs? In other words, the employees must be able to align the job responsibilities with their values, beliefs, morals, and ethical judgments and responsibilities. Empowered employees must be caring, idealistic, and do the job to the standard that has been established by the organization. In other words, will they want to make decisions concerning a guest/customer request within their job responsibility, or wait for the manager while the guest/customer is waiting?

Aptitude

Do the employees have the aptitude to perform this new responsibility with their skill levels? In general, employees possess the temperament, judgment, and have the capability to do their job as a result of proper training. Then, they should be allowed to solve problems and make certain decisions. Empowered employees feel a sense of worth and competency.

Autonomy

The employees must have a sense of independence if they are to succeed in this endeavor. The leader must facilitate and encourage risk taking to a certain extent. This will be further discussed below in types of empowerment. But, employees must be allowed to make some decisions and allow room for mistakes and corrections. Or else, they will never learn to be independent. Self-determined employees feel they can control the decision making process and should be allowed to room to do so.

Impact

Do the employees know that the new power they are about to take has direct impact on the success or failure of the organization? You as the leader should lead this discussion. They should know that by assuming this new power, whatever decision they make will have an impact on the company's bottom line, because it will determine whether the guest/customer will return.

Iverson (2001) believes that most employees would prefer to work in organizations that grant autonomy, and employees prefer empowerment for the following reasons:

- People are smarter and more capable than we assume they are.
- Everyone wants to be treated as an adult.
- We all want to be consulted before decisions that affect us.
- Nearly everyone wants to do an outstanding job and is proud of their work.
- We want to be trusted and have greater authority and freedom at work.

Before you commit yourself to empowering others, you must decide to what extent you are willing to go. Unilateral empowerment without guidelines may not be effective, and may become another fire you will be extinguishing. The following are four basic levels of empowerment.

Flexible

With flexible empowerment, employees are given broad powers to please and satisfy their guests/customers. Employees are allowed to do whatever is necessary to please the guests/customers by taking actions, or even spending some dollar amounts. For example, at the Walt Disney World resort, the Cast Members are empowered to make a Guest Service Recovery by using "No Strings Attached Policy." The Cast Members, irrespective of their line of business, are empowered to please any guest that is inconvenienced. You may be in merchandise department, and noticed a young guest drops her ice cream or beverage. With no string attached policy, that Cast Member will issue that guest (or any adult with her) a coupon to redeem another ice cream or beverage in the nearest restaurant of their choice. If the Walt Disney World resort is to remain the number one tourist destination in the world, the most "Magical" place to visit, and if the "Magic" is to be preserved, it must ensure its Cast Members some measure of empowerment. I believe it has done this effectively.

Also at Ritz Carlton, every level of Ladies and Gentlemen is empowered to spend up to $2000 to satisfy a guest that is dissatisfied, or wow an important guest. The guests of Ritz Carlton come there for one or two particular reasons: expects the best, the same quality products, and impeccable service. Ritz-Carlton models part of its to be "Ladies and Gentlemen serving Ladies and Gentlemen." If the service standard is to remain that way, then, empowerment is an absolute.

Individual

This type of empowerment is given to an individual with certain responsibilities. As an individual responsible for a particular job, you are empowered to make decisions within that job description. For example, if you are a front desk agent, you may be empowered to deal with any guest complains that has direct link to your job; such as check-in/check- out, room changes, and/or room discounts. The power of the employee is within the realm of the front desk alone. Another example is a wait staff that is empowered to compliment guest/customer meals, replace any item, or give discounts.

Team

Team empowerment could encompass team within a department or a group of people; these are *self-directed work teams*, appointed to solve a problem. As it was with the front desk agent, a team empowerment will be members of the front office. These include the employees of the front desk, bell staff, valet parking, and concierge. In other words, any member of this team is empowered to satisfy any guest with any concern regarding the front office. The *self-directed work team* works as an independent team. This type of team comprises employees from different departments, and is made up of both managers and hourly employees. It is like an ad hoc team put together with the responsibility "to solve a problem, improve processes, or take on responsibilities normally reserve for management such as hiring, scheduling, and evaluating" (Iverson, 2001, p. 329).

Structured

Structured empowerment gives employees guidelines on what to do to please and make guests/customers happy. It is very structured that employees have steps and guidelines they must take when making guest/customer recovery. Sometimes it could be very frustrating on the side of the employees because it is an old style, sticking to the manager's rule and a way the manager can still keep control. For instance, a guest complains about their steak, the wait staff would want to know the specific problem with the steak. And if it is possible to get another steak, or a replacement item, or a discount, and may be finally decides to compliment the meal. In this rapid-in-and-out hospitality environment, the employee may be frustrated due to lack of time. You may also have a customer that is not very happy with the slow pace of recovery. Positively speaking, it only gives employees step-by-step guidelines to follow; it is not more effective than any other types of empowerment.

Empowerment is the process of allowing employees to make decision within their job responsibility. Empowerment can be beneficial in following ways:

- Even though through empowerment manager are giving up power, it sharpen the manager's leadership skills by allowing the employees to participate in a democratic way.
- Empowerment makes dependent employees independent and less reliant on others.
- Empowerment can be a motivation and a way to improve employee efficiency.
- If properly implemented, empowerment could improve organizational effectiveness.
- Empowerment helps employee become better problem solvers and decision makers.

We have all heard the word delegation. At times, we have interchangeably used delegation instead of empowerment, and vise versa. Delegation can be used effectively by managers and leaders; or it can be misused by dumping insignificant task on the employees. When you hear your manager telling you what to do, directing you, yelling out what you are doing wrong, and telling you how many long hours he spends everyday at work, then you know he has no delegating skills. Since you are the manager and responsible for the output of your people and operations, it is necessary that you hire the right people and develop them to delegate some of your responsibilities to them, while you keep some to yourself. The manager has varying degrees of responsibilities. Responsibilities such as scheduling, inventory, order and receiving, checking mailbox, and returning certain phone call can be delegated. While tasks such as hiring, termination, interviewing, discipline, reprimand, and evaluation can be performed by the manager. Delegation is giving some your responsibilities to you competent employees. Delegation is no abdication of duties.

Many leaders, especially the Theory X leaders, unfortunately there are still many of them in the hospitality industry today who do not believe in delegation. Why would Theory X leaders who believe employees are lazy, hate work, want to be coerced would want to delegate? No reasons! These leaders would not want to do it, and if they attempt to delegate, it will be a disaster that may lead to frustrations. Some other reasons some leader do not delegate are:

Lack of faith in their employees
Most managers have no faith in the ability of their employees. The simple belief of allowing the employees to use their potential to achieve success is not there. This may happen because of past experience; however, no bad experience is too hard to overcome.

Lack of confidence in themselves
Some managers fear the employee may do the job better than them, and thereby lose respect before other employees. If this actually

happens, it could lead to several questions of how the manager will handle himself. The manager could develop some fears and start to ask himself some tough questions such as: how could I answer to manager? How could I reprimand employees for poor performances? How can I coach poor performing employees? How can I approach employee without confidence when I have non myself? These fears actually do exist.

Some are promoted through the ranks.

Moving from hourly to management positions could be a difficult transition for many people. Many managers may slip back to what is called **boomerang management**: that is doing the work themselves because of the ease and the convenience.

Some managers believe their constant presence is important.

It is important to be visible; however some managers believe their constant presence is required for the success of their operations, and like to be in control. This seems to be a problem of ego. Maybe if they have the courage to step aside and watch their employees do their thing, they will be amazed how less important their presence maybe.

Fear of giving up or losing their power.

Delegation is a means of losing some of your powers. So, some managers believe if they delegate, there goes the power and their only means of control: so, they will not delegate. They feel by not delegating, they will increase their power and hold on to it.

For one reason or another, managers want to be in the loop all the time.

Some mangers want to be in-the-know all the time. This is simply not going to happen, if only they know so, but they do not. This is simply a way to protect their personal interest and not that of the operations.

While some leaders may assume their own mistakes, they would not take responsibility for others.

Some managers do not want to assume anyone employee's mistakes, or be dependent on their employees. They may not know what the possible outcome would be if the employee does not go through with the responsibility. They fear negative reactions from their peers and managers.

Why delegate when I can do it faster?

They believe it is faster to get the job done than to delegate it. If it takes the supervisor 30 minutes to do the schedule, why does the task need to be delegated to someone else? If it takes 5 minutes to enter the sales for the day, why delegate it?

Desire for personal recognition

They want all the accolades and recognitions. They desire nothing but personal gains, sharing the rewards with others is not necessary, so they will do it all themselves to look good in presence of their manager and employees.

The hospitality industry is very intense, stressful, fast pace, and could burn you out fast. The physical and emotional stress comes as a result of working longer hours and performing tasks that could be detrimental your health. Below are some symptoms of burnout.

Symptoms of Burnout

- Feeling agitated
- Beginning to hate the job
- Irritated by other staff members
- Chest pain
- Difficulty sleeping

- Loss of appetite
- Low enthusiasm/energy
- Passes out on the job
- Physical ailments
- Physical exhaustion

- Distrustful of other staff members
- Emotional exhaustion
- Excessive eating
- Heart problem
- Impatient with others
- Lack of motivation

- Poor decision making
- Stomach pains
- Feeling stressed
- Ulcers
- Walks out of the job

Source: Cliff Goodwin, Alfred B. Squire III, & Elwood Chapman, (2005). "*The hospitality supervisor's survival kit.*" Upper Saddle River, NJ: Prentice Hall, Inc.

Any supervisor that begins to feel any of these symptom or going through some of the conditions above may want to seek medical help. As part of a larger perspective, it is time for the supervisor to start sharing the work load.

Delegation can be effective if it is properly implemented. After all, the purpose of delegation is to get a task done by a lower level employee. The manager should facilitate the process effectively because the end result will be a reflection of its delegation skills.

Plan ahead

You need to look ahead to see how your day, week, or month will look like and schedule your time effectively. You start by listing the tasks you perform on a regular basis, and sort them into two groups: 1) varying degree of difficulties, 2) what to delegate and what should not be delegated. Define the assignments in clear terms and simplify it for clear understanding for anyone to grasps the simple concept. The next step is selecting the appropriate employee to delegate the assignment.

Choose the right employee

This is the key ingredient that will make it or break it. It is necessary to select the right person that will perform this task. You should talk to the employees by calming their worries and concerns. Also, help them put away their fears. This employee should have the competency, skill, drive, determination, and commitment for the job. Delegation does not just occur; it is an agreement between you and the employee. Once the employee accepts the responsibility, it becomes a contract.

Clarify the range of discretion

At this stage, you let the employee know the area of responsibility, discretions, and limits. You clarify your goals, performance standard and expectant results. Specify and communicate the authority the employee will need to do the job. For instance, specify the kind of decision to be made independently, decisions with consultations, and how much money can be spent, the items on the menu to be discounted or complemented, if necessary.

Communicate to those it will affect

Now, you have decided on what task to delegate, the employee to delegate it to, and ranges of authority to get the job done. After this, you communicate it to the specific employee that will perform the task, and other employees this decision will affect. Everyone needs to be in the loop as to what has been delegated, to whom it was delegated, the range of authority, and those it will affect. Failure to inform others may result in conflict and failure, leading to confusion and inability of the employee to successfully complete the task.

Follow-up

It is the responsibility of managers to train their employees as needed. You go through the whole process of what you want done, who to do it, how it should be done, when it should be done, and when it should be completed. Then communicate this to everyone so that all those concern will be in the loop. If this does not happen, there will be **reverse delegation**. This is when the employees dump the assignment back you to perform. This happens when the employee experiences most or all the reasons employees refuse delegation (see below). To prevent reverse delegation from occurring, practice the principle of: Do Not Bring Me Problems, Bring Me Solutions (DNBMP/BMS). This works all the time.

Most workers in the hospitality industry are part time and are barely able to do their jobs with less supervision. A good number of the part time employees are in the industry to make a buck or two to make ends meet, not necessarily in their chosen profession. These are not the type of employees you want to delegate assignments. Of those employees who are dedicated, below are some of the reasons they will refuse delegation.

Fear of failure

Some the employees fear failure just as some managers do. They fear the response from their peers and manager when they fail to perform and meet the expected result. Rather than face humiliation and scorn, they will refuse any form of delegation.

Rejection by their peers

Peer pressure and rejection is another reason. The employees worry about what names they will be called by their peers. They believe they might be perceived as defecting to the side of management and will no longer be seen as part of the clique by their peers.

Improper training

Many employees may not have the necessary training and skills for the assign responsibility. The employees are barely making an impact in their jobs, assigning them a management responsibility is a far stretch.

Lack of confidence

Just as some managers lack confidence in themselves, so are some employees. They are dependent on others to get their work done and do not want to make any mistakes that could make them feel or be seen as incompetent.

No interest in climbing the corporate ladder

Many employees are satisfied with the status quo, they are happy and do not intend to move further than where they are. They see their work as a job that pays the bill and are happy with it.

Responsibility is meaningless and without reward or incentive

Many would not take on additional responsibility if there is nothing in there for them. This could be as a result of past experience where by the manager dumps work on them, and offers no reward or incentive. This is called ***job loading*** and should be avoided as much as possible.

Lack of proper support

Lastly, who will take on a responsibility when the manager does not offer any support or encouragement? No one! Some managers do not even say thank you for a job well done, so no employee would take on added responsibility for any manager that shows no appreciation.

Managers delegate because they need more time to manage and lead. Other benefits include the following:

More time to coach

There are 24 hours a day and seven day a week. Managers put in as many hours as necessary to accomplish our work. If you delegate effectively, you will have more time to fall back into coaching role. Leaders should do more coaching than anything else. By delegating and freeing up some time, you will give the employee much deserve time, and coach them on proper ways to perform their jobs. You also use your time effectively in getting other things of importance done.

More employees are trained and development

Through delegation, you will have a group of well trained, skilled, and knowledgeable employees. This will put the employees' potentials to work for the benefit of the organization. This will open opportunities for these employees to explore as they grow and develop in their respective positions. The more people you to develop and train; the more motivated they will be in having job satisfaction and enrichment.

Improve decision making

Decision are easier to reach and make because it is pushed down corporate ladder, rather than coming from the top to the bottom. The decision makers (employees) are closer to the real problems, they are equipped in the process for making decisions, and respond quickly. The employees will have a sense of autonomy, significance, and the belief that they are contributing significantly to the success of their organization.

Employee commitment

Delegation improves employee commitment. The employees will feel more important when they know that they can make decisions that have an impact on the operations. Furthermore, employees will enthusiastically embrace any opportunity for them to make a decision personally than that coming from the top. Employees will be more committed to their job when given this opportunity.

Improves leader-employee relationship

By delegating, the leader demonstrates trust and confidence in the employees. This act leads to better improved interpersonal relationship between the leader and the employees. Both sides are able to share some certain information that may not have been shared if this element of trust had not been expressed.

*"Empowerment is all about letting go
so that others can get going."
– Kenneth Blanchard*

Empowerment and delegation is an effective tool to share the work among every employee. Empowerment helps the employee because they learn how to make decisions and think for themselves. It helps the leader because it frees the leaders time and can concentrate on other people or things that require immediate attention. Delegation on the other hand strengthens the leader's effectiveness. By delegating, the leader is sharing his work with the employees, and preparing some of them to see some of the challenges they may be facing when they decide to ask for that management position. By delegating, the leader is able to use his social intelligent skills in identifying the employees that are competent to perform certain responsibilities. By delegating, the employees learn new skills; you are doing other things such as coaching less competent employees and spending time with the guests.

Accountability
Authority
Boomerang management
Employee
Flexible
Impact
Independence
Individual
Proficiency
Responsibility
Reverse delegation
Sense
Structured
Team

1. Why is delegation important to the supervisor?
2. Discuss in details the three aspects of delegation.
3. Why are these three aspects of delegation important?
4. Which leadership style is more compatible with delegation?
5. Why is delegation less effective with theory X leaders?
6. List some reasons why supervisors do not like to delegate.
7. Certain conditions are necessary for delegations while some are not. Why condition would you say is necessary for delegation?
8. Do you like to delegate? If yes, why? If no, why not?
9. Why is effective communication an important aspect of delegation?
10. Why do you think supervisors do not like to delegate?

CHAPTER SIX

Leading a Diverse Workforce

"Diversity: the art of thinking independently together."
– Malcolm Forbes

What is diversity? Why practice diversity? **Diversity** is the differences in people such as culture, age, sex, income, or race. Diversity is what distinguishes one person from another. It should not be seen as an obstacle, but "an opportunity" (Miller et al., 2007, p. 82).

Every organization has a human resources department that is responsible for interviewing, recruiting, and selecting employees for all of the positions within the organization. Such a department is also charged with protecting employees and adhering to labor laws as they apply to organizations. In recent years, Richard (2000) argued that the role of human resources has moved from a micro relationship to more of a macro relationship. Richard (2000) assumes that a micro relationship focuses on organizational policies and their influences on employee satisfaction, while macro relationships shift from a focus on employees to the organization. This orientation is concerned with how organizational policies shape individual behavior and how this affects an organization's profit. Macro relationships also involve the diversity composition of a workforce, and it is assumed that managing diversity is a continuous process that requires effort, employees' participation, and management's is involvement.

Von Bergen and Soper (2002) define diversity management as "administering social environment and systems, along with organizational climate and procedures, but also entails recognizing, being open to, and utilizing human differences" (p. 239). Managing a diverse team can seem complicated and confusing, but proper rules of conduct, open communication, and respecting employees can make it easier. DeVoe (1999) outlines some issues that can arise when managing diverse staff. The first is creating an environment free of implications relative to managing attitudes. This includes removing any impediments and obstacles such as hostility, viewing everyone as the same, inability for managers to understand differences in culture, and lack of concern for all employees (Iverson, 2001). The second issue focuses on how to work with people from a variety of cultures, backgrounds, and lifestyles. Thirdly, managing a diverse staff requires the ability to manage conflict arising among people of different cultures. One problem for organizational leaders in this new millennium may be how to successfully provide a place for diversity due to the projected increase in minority population in the United States by the U.S Census Bureau.

As the United States population becomes more diverse, so will the hospitality industry. The fastest growing segment of the US population is the minority. The fastest growing minority population is the Hispanic. Almost one in every four American has an African, Asian, Hispanic or Native American ancestry, and this number is expected to change to one in three and two by 2020 and 2050 respectively (Miller et al. 2007).

The hospitality industry has a diverse workforce that will continue to change alongside the changing demography of the United States. According to the 2005 Fact Sheet reported by the National Restaurant Association, foreign-born workers accounted for more than four out of every 10 employees. Furthermore, one out of four eating and drinking establishments (24 %) is minority-owned, and about 23 % is owned by women (National Restaurant Association, 2005).

Salomon and Schork (2003) wrote of women:
> American women comprise 50 % of the population and controls around 80 % of the household spending, buying 81 % of all products and services and writing
>
> 80 % of all checks. A diverse workforce is needed to bring different perspective on the development of products to this important customer base. (p. 40)

Table 6.1

Primary Dimensions	Secondary Dimensions
• Culture – Learned behaviors, arts, beliefs that are taught within a community of people.	• Marital status – A stage indicating whether someone is married or single.
• Ethnicity – Designation of a group of people with common heritage, customs, characteristics, language, or history.	• Education – A process whereby knowledge, skills, mind, and or character is being developed formally or informally.

- Gender – An orientation either assumed by an individual, or it given by people or community.

- Sexual orientation – Behavior associated with the choice and selection of sexual preference.

- Age – This denotes the number of years you have lived.

- Religion – The belief in a higher power or authority.

- Race – Refers to a group of people either related by a common drop of blood, or having the same skin color.

- Language – A distinct tongue of communication between people.

- Physical abilities and qualities – The skills of being able to do something at varying degrees.

- Life experiences – Different stages, knowledge, and understanding humans go through in life.

- Sex – The anatomic composition that determines whether someone is a male or a female.

- Family status – Social unit that comprises the parents and their children, people of the same descent, clan, ancestor, or lineage.

- Income – Earnings received as a result of providing services or labor.

- Power – Authority earned or given to control, influence, rule and command.

- Social status – A position, rank, or a state of affairs occupied within a society.

As the merits and demerits of diversity initiatives are being studied, organizational leaders are being urged to celebrate, embrace, or acknowledge such diversity (Soni, 2000). About 60% of the front-line employees in the hospitality industry are ethnic minorities, which include African American, Hispanic, and Asian-American. As the workforce continues to grow and become even more diverse, the ability of any organization leader to manage this change may determine its ability to compete on a national and global level (Soni, 2000). According to experts, more women, immigrants, and older workers will enter the workforce than in the past. This change is very evident in the hospitality industry (Soni, 2000).

Organizations establish a highly specialized organizational unit when embarking on diversity initiatives. They want to put leaders at ease and spread the workload among those who are not usually consulted for decision making, thus sending a message to employees that the diversity initiative will be taken seriously (Baytos, 1995, p. 95). Baytos (1995) emphasized that whether diversity initiatives are being implemented by a unit or combination of units within the organization, he identified diversity task force, employee diversity council, and employee advocacy/affinity groups as strategic approaches for implementing diversity initiatives.

Diversity Task Force. Task forces are formed at every organizational level, and charged with the responsibility of implementing organizational initiatives. They are usually a small group of between 8 and 15, with half or more of the membership from line and middle managers, and a senior executive member (Baytos, 1995, p. 95). The diversity task force mission is to develop a vision and strategy for the diversity initiatives and develop a business case for the efforts (Baytos, 1995). Its key responsibilities include identification of primary diversity issues, recommend priorities for addressing these issues, serve as diversity champions and models of effective behaviors, and provide feed back to the executive committees on progress, emerging diversity issues, and competitive trends that may affect the organization's efforts.

Baytos (1995) outlines the following specific action steps for a successful diversity task force as:

a) Selecting participants who have personal interest and who commit to make the time available to contribute meaningfully; b) provide the task force with a clear and accountabilities along with a timetable for the achievement of key action steps; c) encouraging task force to broader employee input about the nature and severity of the issues as perceived by employees; and d) when selecting women and minorities to the task force, do not bas any choice on the degree of comfort that the white male officers has with an individual, or on how successfully an individual has been assimilated into the company. (p. 99)

Employee Diversity Council. Baytos (1995) believes that organizations which have between 20 to 30 employees and embrace diversity will use this approach. Its mission will be to identify strategies and tactics that the organization can implement to create individual and cultural diversity that are accepted and valued, open lines of communication among all levels of employees, and provide opportunities to all employees to achieve their career goals (Baytos, 1995). The tone of the council should be "differences are welcome and to be understood, and that all inputs have values" (p. 96). The main responsibility of the employee diversity council is to identify policies, programs, and practices that need revision to meet the needs of the workforce. To accomplish it mission, it will rely on personal experiences of members of the council, as well as inputs from the general workforce within the organization.

Action steps to ensuring a successful employee diversity council according to Baytos (1995) include:

a) appointment of council members by the chief executive officer;

b) a well written, clear, and realistic mission statement; c) provide training to council members at an early stage regarding diversity; d) formation of subcommittees within the council to focus on specific areas; e) participants are cautioned about long-term nature of the effort, and the need for both commitment and patience; and f) a formal linkage is made between the council and human resources staff. (p 97)

Employee Advocacy/Affinity Groups. The diversity task force and employee diversity council are approaches conceived by the top management of the organizations, and are implemented as top-down decision making process. While the employee advocacy/ affinity groups are a bottom-up phenomenon (Baytos, 1995). Membership within this group is usually large as they are drawn from individuals of like race or gender grouping. It could sometimes including a functional twist such as "black employees, Hispanic employees, minority engineers, career moms, female employees, Asian employees, women in management, and gay and lesbian alliances" (Baytos, 1995, p. 96). Its mission statement may be to help its members with career networking and an advisory task force to senior management and the human resources department. Main responsibility may be to identify the areas of the organization where the climate is not very supportive of its members, band together to provide mutual support, and draw attention to issues of fair treatment.

To have a successful advocacy group, Baytos (1995) believes that management should:

a) support the existence of the group, or at least recognize the validity of employees' interests in forming such groups;

b) links should be established with the human resources department so that the employee input is captured, realistic expectations can be established, and competing priorities of various groups can be balanced and sequenced; c) balance attention and resources so that no one group is seen as receiving a disproportionate share of benefits or as having excessive clout; and d) provide groups with education and training to help them develop a broad perspective that goes beyond the needs of their particular group. (p. 97)

"We need diversity of thought in the world to face the new challenges."
– Tim Berners Lee

Many organizations have employees from diverse backgrounds. Such organizations are plural organizations but not necessarily multicultural organizations (Iverson, 2001). Organizations that value its diversity are multicultural organizations. Iverson (2001) stated further that multicultural organization have the following characteristics:

Seeks to diversify both management and line staff by attracting well-qualified majority and non-majority member candidates; an absence of both formal and informal bias within the organization; a proactive management style that minimizes conflict; relies upon all employees, including majority and non-majority group members, for planning, setting goals, decision making, and day-by-day operation of the organization; and the diverse ideas and views of the multicultural staff are sought and valued. (p. 306)

Equal Employment Opportunity. The Civil Rights Act of 1964 and the Equal Employment Opportunity Act of 1972 paved the way for more women and minority entrance into the workforce (Iverson, 2001). Both Acts guarantee individual rights in terms of equal employment without regard to race, color, religion, gender, or national origin. Iverson, (2001) believes this has long standing consequences in diversity management. With organizations quietly condoning subtle discrimination informally, subsequent laws such as The Vocational Rehabilitation Act of 1973, protecting handicapped employees of companies with federal contracts; Age Discrimination Act of 1981, protecting individuals between the ages of forty and seventy; and Americans with Disabilities Act of 1991, protecting persons with disabilities within both the private and public sector (Iverson, 2001). By law, organizations must adhere to Equal Employment Opportunity guidelines when hiring, selecting, promoting, and dismissing employees (Iverson, 2001).

Affirmative Action. This policy resulted from two executive orders from President Lyndon Johnson, designed to increase employment opportunities for women, minorities, veterans and the handicapped. Affirmative action means "the explicit use of a person's group identity as a criterion in making selection decision" (Iverson, 2001, p. 307). The two strategies supporting the programs are the good faith effort strategy and the quota system strategy.

The good faith strategy is supposed to assure that women, minorities, and other groups are equally represented in the workforce compared, to actual availability in the population. This can be achieved by placing ads in newspapers that can reach the target population. The guidelines only applied to organizations doing business with the federal government. Should companies fail to meet the quotas of protected groups, they must either improve the number or lose federal funding and contracts (Iverson, 2001). The quota system requires the percentage of any minority group in the population to be reflected in the organizations workforce. This sometimes led to non-selection of a majority candidate who was equally qualified for that position. Legal cases such as *United States v. Weber* (1979), the court rejected the case of a white employee who claimed that the company practiced reverse discrimination because the company set aside 50 % of its training positions for minorities. In other cases such as, *Firefighters Local No 1784 v. Scott* (1984) and *Wagant v. Jackson Board of Education,* (1986), the courts rejected racial preference (Schramm, 2003). Many private organizations, through their own initiative have adopted affirmative action programs. Several human resources managers through recruiting process have developed a statistical process for monitoring groups. Schramm (2003) contends that:

> Before the U.S. Supreme Court's recent upholding affirmative action at the University of Michigan, many companies had expressed support for affirmative action programs, it's not surprising. Business sees diversity as crucial for building competitiveness. In a world of vast population diversity, companies feel it is crucial that workforce reflect customers they serve. This emphasis is unlikely to change as ethnic minorities' proportion of the population continues to grow. (p.192)

Diversity Awareness Training. Equal employment opportunity and affirmative action programs may reduce or even eliminate totally both formal and informal organizational biases; they may never eliminate individual biases. Many organizations take steps to adopt diversity programs. Unfortunately, many of the programs fail because they are not pursued with the same amount of energy and zeal that directly affect the companies' bottom line. Diversity awareness training is not a one time workshop by a hired expert, or showing of a video purchased off-the-shelf (Iverson, 2001).

Although many diversity consultants may consider themselves experts in diversity training and awareness, Iverson (2001) argues that one of the key successes to diversity training "consists of several days of programming designed to teach managers and employees skills to build effective, culturally diverse teams" (p. 309). Furthermore, Bendick, Jr., Egan, and Lofhjelm (2001) believe that a comprehensive approach to diversity training is ingrained in the theory of organizational development by focusing on this nine training practices.

First, *training has strong support from the top management.* That is senior executives and managers must show the employees their total commitment to the issue of diversity by being the first to endorse and attend training, repeatedly referring to its lessons and applying lessons learned, and echoing the diversity issues in employee performance coaching and evaluations.

Secondly, *training is tailored to each client organization.* An off-the-shelf training package is insufficient to provide the minimum training on diversity issues for the training to be considered successful.

Thirdly, *training links diversity to central operating goals.* Training is not provided merely to address an incident or a conscience or individuals. Organizations must undertake training as a way to advance its most important operational goals through increased productivity, reduced costs, easier recruitment enhanced creativity, improved client service, and an expanded market base.

Fourth, *trainers are managerial or organization development professionals.* They must have experience with organizational management, be educated in leadership, and be able to relate their experiences to the situations.

Fifth, *training enrolls all levels of employees.* Involving every level of employee from senior executives to frontline supervisors is essential because of their various rules in the decision making process.

Sixth, *training discusses discrimination as a general process.* It emphasizes both psychological and social processes that address inclusion and exclusion, stereotype, in-group and out-group bias, social comfort, and group thinking.

Seventh, *training explicitly addresses individual behavior.* Training being provided must actively engage trainees in developing and practicing new habits of speaking and acting more likely to influence post-training behavior.

Eighth, *training is complemented by changes in human resources practice.* The training addresses basic supervisory skills for new and inexperienced managers, in how to deal with communication and interpersonal conflicts.

Ninth, *training impacts the corporate culture.* The incorporation of all these benchmarks combined with organizational self-examination, symbolic acts, reforms of policies and procedures, and selective changes in personnel to achieve far reaching changes, will enhance the organizational beliefs, values, and an inclusive work environment.

> *"We need to reach that happy stage of our development when differences and diversity are not seen as sources of division and distrust, but of strength and inspiration."*
> *– Josefa Iloilo*

Diversity is good business. Period! As the US population increases, so does minority population. There are a lot of women and minorities in this industry, and their needs cannot be ignored. The best approach is to be proactive and be attentive to the needs of the diverse workers. Progressive organizations do embrace diversity and inclusiveness, because they know this is one of the ways to show their appreciation for their employees. Encourage cultural interactions, cultural awareness training, sensitivity training, and teach inclusive communication.

Affirmative Action
Age
Culture
Diverse Workforce
Diversity Awareness Training
Diversity Task Force
Education
Employee Advocacy/Affinity Groups
Employee Diversity Council
Equal Employment Opportunity
Ethnicity
Family status
Gender
Income
Language
Life experiences
Marital status
Multicultural Organization
Physical abilities and qualities
Power
Primary Dimensions
Race
Religion
Secondary Dimensions
Sex
Sexual orientation
Social status

1. What is your definition of diversity? How is this different from the definition in your text?

2. Have you ever faced discrimination? If yes, how did feel about it? If no, how do you think you will feel if you experience discrimination?

3. Why do you think diversity is necessary in the workplace?

4. Why do you think diversity is an absolute in the hospitality industry?

5. List some steps that are necessary to develop cross-cultural awareness.

6. How would you encourage diversity initiatives in your organization?

7. List six diversity issues. Which of the issues are the most important to you?

8. Do you prefer to interact with people form your own culture? Why?

9. Are there any groups you would rather not any form of interactions? Why?

10. List and discuss with your class some of your traditions and customs.

CHAPTER SEVEN

Leading Marginal Employee

*"Effective leadership is putting first things first.
Effective management is discipline, carrying it out."*
– Stephen Covey

If there is one task managers do not like to do, it is discipline! Even though this is one of the responsibilities managers have. Before you decide to discipline any employee, it is important to determine if that employee understands why the discipline process is taking place. In other words, "discipline is a process that aims to clarify, correct, and improve inappropriate job-related conduct and behavior through rewards and sometimes penalties" (Drummond, 1990, p. 260). Discipline is necessary to conduct a state of order. If everyone knows the rules and proper conduct established in the place of work, and the leaders empowered to enforce these rule do it correctly, disciplining employees could be done in a more positive environment. However, if employees do not follow the rules and procedures, or do not even know what rule and procedures exist for in their place of work, discipline could be more problematic than the word itself. If employees themselves have the self-discipline and a positive climate is created, all the leaders of the organization have to do is reverse to coaching role which will help both the employees and the leaders.

The 10 deadly sins found in reprimanding employees

1. Lacking a complete understanding of the rules and/or not making them clear to others.
2. Ignoring the seriousness of an offense as well as any mitigating and aggravating circumstances.
3. Failing to get all relevant facts and acting on hearsay evidence.
4. Procrastinating in taking action against violations.
5. "Flying off the handle" or losing one's temper.
6. Being unclear in letting the other person know that the precise offence is for which he or she is being punished.
7. Not getting the other person's point of view or interpretation of the facts.
8. Letting the subordinate talk the manager out of the punishment.
9. Failing to maintain some record of what has gone on, why the punishment was given, and what the next step will be if the matter is not corrected.
10. Nursing a grudge or "holding it against the employee" for having had to be discipline.

Source: Schwartz, A. E. (1995). Counseling the marginal performer. CPA Journal, 65(2), 66-67.

Changing employee behavior starts from the day you interview them with the purpose of hiring them to be a part of your organization. Before deciding to discipline an employee, you should ask yourself some of these questions:

1. Does the employee have the company's code of conduct?
2. Has the employee signed any document expressing understanding of the behavior?
3. Does the employee know the company policy?
4. Does the employee know that the behavior is not tolerated?

All these questions need to be considered before you forge ahead with any form of discipline. Before you decide to discipline an employee, you should also determine if that behavior is changeable within the environment you have created. Irrespective of how difficult is it to approach employees about their behavior or attitude, it is better if actions are taken immediately than later. Taking action later could have a far reaching negative effect on the employee, peers, the leadership, operation, and organization.

Identify the behavior/performance
We cannot change people; neither should we tell them to change themselves. So, it is important to make sure that when it comes to discipline, the leader is identifying a behavior that can be changed by the employee. You may tell an employee about their mode of interactions with fellow employees and the guests/customers, their attitude towards the job, their perception about each other. All these behaviors can be changed because it could have a direct impact on the organization and the bottom line. However, you cannot tell the employee to stop smoking, or become whatever you think they should. When it comes to performance, identify it and be specific. The performance in question should be measurable and quantified. In other words, it should be a performance issue the employee could improve. For instance, reducing the speed of making a Chicken Caesar Salad from three minutes to two minutes; or reducing the speed of guest check-in from four minutes to two minutes. These performances can be improved.

Talk to employees in private

Once you have identified the behavior or performance, call a private meeting and discuss it with the employee. Do everything you can to keep it as confidential as possible, and to prevent other employees from finding out about the disciplinary process to avoid any embarrassment it might cause. Believe it or not, your trust, respect, and integrity is on the line.

Watch your emotions

Emotions are important part of us, but as managers and leaders, we cannot let this be a part of us when we deal with employees during discipline. You should not show your emotions, especially negatively when you are in the process of disciplining your employees. Your emotions should be checked as they may not be appropriate at this particular time. If you express your emotions and be come negative, all the employee will remember is your emotions and the subject of the moment will be lost. Never discipline an employee when you are angry, remain calm, take control of your emotions, and be objective.

Talk, and then listen

At the time of discipline, you are inviting the employee to a discussion about a problem, and not the time to lecture. If you go into the lecturing mode, you will over talk the employee. Having told the employee why you invited him into your office, also tell the employee why you are worried, then listen to the employee to understand where the employee is coming from, and why he does what you are concern about. You are not only getting their side of the story, but getting them involved in solving the problem. After all, it is the employee that has the problem and probably the only one that has the best solution to it.

Seek commitment

Since we cannot change anyone, or tell people what to do and not do, we as leaders must facilitate an environment where positive behavior must strive. After discussing with the employee about the behavior in question, seek to gain their commitment. Before leaving, ask the employee to summarize the discussion you have just had, to make sure there is understanding on both sides. Seek the employee commitment to change the behavior and have it documented with the employee signature on it.

Follow-up

Set dates and time for follow-up to assess the employee's progress. A time convenient to both sides should be determined. More so, let the employee know that if the behavior continues, this meeting could happen sooner than agreed upon date. This is when you decide to use one of the two discipline approaches (progressive/negative or positive discipline). This may depend on your leadership style, or the discipline approach of your organization. Before departing, express your confidence in the employee, and reaffirm that you are there to help in case of any challenges.

7 pitfalls for managers when handling poor performers and how to overcome them

Pitfall 1: Utilizing a punitive versus a corrective approach.
Pitfall 2: Assuming that the employee will somehow disappear without your having to do anything.
Pitfall 3: Allowing legal concerns to dictate your course of action.
Pitfall 4: Not hearing the employee out.
Pitfall 5: Setting, low standards and expectations for employees.
Pitfall 6: Performance reviews do not accurately reflect performance deficiencies.
Pitfall 7: Making documentation harder than it really is.

Source: Scott, M. (2000). 7 pitfalls for managers when handling poor performers and how to overcome them. *Manage*

Discipline can be approached both positively and progressively or negatively. The organizational culture and environment will usually determine the type of discipline to implement.

Positive discipline is a new trend of leading marginal employees successfully. It is a way of placing the conduct and behavior of the employees in the employees' hands, and asking them to find the appropriate ways to correct their actions. In other words, instead of warning the employees about their actions, the employees are reminded of the standard and their commitment to the organization. Positive discipline should be facilitated in the following ways.

Stage one – Oral reminder

In this stage, you point out the employee's infraction as you see it happen, but in a friendly and positive manner. After pointing it out to the employee, let the employee speak and listen to what the employee has to say. Express you confident in the employee and ask the employee to find a corrective way to prevent the action from repeating itself in the future. You may make notes of this discussion in your own calendar, and let the employee know that you are doing this for your own records.

Stage two – Written reminder

This will happen if the action continues to repeat itself. You will call the employee to your office for a private and serious discussion. At this point, you will speak in the affirmative and be assertive. Be sure to secure a commitment from the employee that this action will not repeat itself in the future. Reaffirm to the employee that everyone within the organization must be in compliant with company's policy. Do not forget that your role is that of a coach and a counselor (Theory Y). Have this discussion documented with your signature and the employee's signature. If necessary, get witnesses to be signatories to this document, and place it in the employees file. Again, reaffirm your confidence in the employee that this action will not be repeated in the future.

Stage three – Suspension with pay

At this stage, the action has probably repeated itself three times. This is the time to have a more serious discussion with the employee about his action. You may decide to send the employee home with pay for a few days to reflect on his actions. While at that, the employee should ponder some questions such as: how important is my job? How relevant am I to the organization? How important is my career? How much conformity do I need to have to keep my job? When the employee returns to work, the employee will return with a written statement that states the action, promises that the action will not repeat itself in the future, and if it does, it will be met with more serious consequence which could be as severe as termination. The statement should have three signatures: one for the employee, one for you, and the last for a witness. After signing the document, it should be placed in the employee's permanent file. What you have done here is given the employee a rope to hang himself. Again, reaffirm your confident in the employee, because you are a coach and a counselor.

Stage four – Termination/resignation

If the employee does not live up to the written statement he has produced himself, the employee loses his job: period. However, how the employee leaves the employment maybe decided by you. Do you terminate the employee outright or do you allow the employee to turn-in a two-week notice? The call is yours as the leader. If you however decide to allow the employee to turn in two weeks notice, let the employee leave and pay him for the two weeks. A distraught employee may become destructive and cause some damage of monetary significant to the company. It will be wiser to pay a few hundred dollars than replace a fryer or a grill costing a few thousand dollars.

In general, organizations using positive approach to discipline get exceptional response from a significant number of their employees. Most employees do not go about breaking company rules. There are honest mistakes which lead to discipline, the approach is what matters. Miller et al. (2007) believe the positive discipline "approached discipline rule breaking as a problem to be solved, not as wrongdoing to be punished. It does not threaten people's self-respect, as punishment does; rather, it enlists their efforts in solving the problem" (p. 324). Everyone, especially employees would like to be treated as adults and be recognized for good performance.

When you ask people what is the definition of discipline, most will say punishment. That means that if you enforce the rules by punishing people for breaking the rules, others will learn to obey them, or they will see punishment as a result of towing the line of obedience. This is compliance through fear. Negative or progressive discipline is used immensely in the hospitality industry; because most managers believe the only way to get employees to comply is by firm, total control, iron-fisted, and autocratic ways (Theory X). This approach does little or nothing to motivate employees. It may result in having difficult employees who have built defense mechanism for disobeying rules. Negative discipline is administered in the following four stages:

Stage one – Oral/verbal warning
In this stage, you are simply stating action of the employee that you are addressing, and warning the employee that this action must not be repeated. There is a written documentation at this stage, indicating your conversation and remedial steps. Even though this is not a punitive action, it is far less friendly than oral reminder (positive discipline).

Stage two – Written warning

At this stage, you are stating that the offense has been repeated again, and punishment will be administered. The action you take here may be dependent on your company policy. Some companies may terminate an employee at this stage. If your company does not terminate at this stage, you will have a written document stating the offense. This document should be signed by you, the employee, and one or two eyewitnesses. If the employee refused to sign, allow the employee to give reasons for refusal to sign. The document should be placed in the employee's file.

Stage three – Suspension

Some companies may terminate at this stage or suspend the employee. Some other companies may suspend without pay between two to three days depending on the severity of the offense. The suspension is also to allow the employee to contemplate what he has done and reflect on the possible consequences. Some employees find suspension with pay as non punitive. Some employers may even pay the employees upon return to work after considering the situation in a different context.

Stage four – Termination

Termination occurs if the action begins to repeat itself after the employee returns to work. The termination should be conducted in private with another manager present. It should be positive and do not show your emotions.

How to effectively deal with a poor performer: Your true test of leadership

- **Think** – Think about the exhibited behavior before confronting to the employee. Try to see the situation from the employee's perspective to understand his motivation....this will also help diffuse your reactive anger.

- **Plan** – Plan what you will say before meeting with the employee. Focus on the situation you observed. Focus specifically on the employee behavior rather than on the employee personality.
- **Picture** – Picture how the employee is going to respond. Imagine the employee's reaction when you discuss his behavior. Do not sugarcoat the anticipated response.
- **Describe** – When you meet with employee describe the behavior you observed. Remember to stay focus on the behavior not the person.
- **Ask** – Ask the employee to explain his action. By doing so you will better understand the reason for the behavior.
- **Listen** – Listen and let the employee do most of the talking. This will most likely be difficult for you. You are used to taking charge of situations and doing the talking.
- **Agree** – Agree on what the desired behavior should be. Review the correct procedure, citing written guidelines.
- **Affirm** – Finally, affirm to him he can do it. Let him know you have confidence.

Source: Evenson, R. (1998). How to effectively deal with a poor performer: Your true test of leadership. *Supervision*, 59(7), 12-14.

Before taking any form of disciplinary actions, be sure to know the limits of your powers, and get your human resources involve in it. Disciplinary action should be taken carefully to avoid and sense of impropriety.

"Right discipline consists, not in external compulsion, but in the habits of mind which lead spontaneously to desirable rather than undesirable activities."
– Bertrand Russell

Discipline is a way to make everyone adhere to company policies and procedures. It is an orderly way to make employees comply with rules. Discipline is not to be mistaken for punishment. Before applying discipline, the situation and employee must be assessed. A good and efficient employee may not need a progressive form of discipline, even if that is the form of discipline applied within the organization. You may follow positive discipline in order to maintain morale and keep a good employee. That does not however mean that a good employee should not be reprimanded for bad behavior. Furthermore, termination should be taken seriously as you are taking someone livelihood away from them. Think whether the situation can be salvaged. Most of the time it can if only the manager addresses the situation before it gets to this stage.

Changing employee behavior
Follow-up
Identify the behavior/performance
Oral reminder
Oral/verbal warning
Positive discipline
Progressive discipline
Seek commitment
Suspension
Suspension with pay
Talk to employees in private
Talk, and then listen
Termination
Termination/resignation
Watch your emotions
Written reminder
Written warning

1. Define discipline. Define marginal employee.
2. Explain in details the four essential of discipline.
3. What is the difference between oral warning and verbal warning?
4. Why is it important to watch your emotions?

5. Determining discipline as a supervisor, to what extent should you consider the circumstances?
6. Compare and contrast progressive and positive approaches to discipline. Which is applicable in your organization? Why?
7. Which approach do you prefer? Why?
8. Why is it important to have documentation before terminating employee?
9. Do you believe any situation is salvable? List some general steps to salvage a situation.
10. Why is discipline important?

CHAPTER EIGHT

Leading by Solving Problems and Making-Decisions

> *"I am enough of an artist to draw freely upon my imagination. Imagination is more important than knowledge. Knowledge is limited. Imagination encircles the world."*
> *– Albert Einstein*

Leaders today must solve problems and make decisions more complex than they have ever faced. These problems could arise as a result of legal, environmental, political, customer complains, inexperience employees, or shortage of skilled workers. For the supervisors in the hospitality industry, the fast-pace, hustling, lack of time and pressure makes it harder to make effective decisions. But, it is still your job to make decisions that will positively impact your operations.

The first aspect of solving problem is identifying the issues that warrant the most attention and considerations. This could be the most difficult aspect of the process. By troubleshooting and going to the source, you will be able to identify what needs attention before problem surfaces. These sources include employee surveys, employees' suggestion box, guests and customer comment cards, focus groups, using a secret shopper, management by walking/wandering around (MBWA), and being aware of your environment.

As you become conscious of your environment, you will begin to examine both your internal and external environments for challenges, concerns, and identifying problems. This will almost become a second nature to you. This is called **environmental scanning**. This is the process of gathering "useful information from the environment that can help you identify and anticipate problems" (Iverson, 2001, p. 54). This is mostly effective for external environment.

Since the hospitality industry is a trendy industry, it is important for you to stay abreast of current trends and developments to be competitive. These trends or development could have a long and lasting effect on your operation. The effect could be negative or positive. You approach, problem solving skills, quick and creative response may make all the difference. Below are four traditional modes of thinking managers use:

Rational thinking

This process involves the use of facts, logic, and reasoning to solve problems and arrive at decisions. Every source used to make this decision can be verified and observed. The information can be extracted from other sources. A good example is your budget. To make budgetary decisions, you have to go through your sales figure from the past, labor costs, inventory, and other sources available to you. Leaders using this process have really researched their sources to assist them to make intelligent and cogent decision.

Impulsive thinking

This process involves making decisions from the cuff, spur of the moment, rather than base it on facts and reasoning. There is little or no thinking involve in this process. For example, a hostess goes to the manager and says "Ms. Johnson is complaining that she arrived 30 minutes ago and has not been seated." The manager responds by saying "get her a table immediately." Only, to later learn that she was only there for lees than 10 minute when she complained. This is a matter of perception. Leaders using this process cannot distinguish between what is important and what is necessary. They are bamboozled, bewildered, bemused, frustrated and puzzled individuals.

Intuitive thinking

This process of problem solving to reach a decision is based on stored information in the memory and past experiences. This is the hunch, gut feeling, sixth sense, or premonition. Let's use the last example of Ms. Johnson, again. On hearing the complaint of Ms. Johnson, the name will ring a bell and the manager will juggle his memory. Based on past experience, the manager knows how to respond and react. Leaders with this type of approach have strong ego, self-esteem, confident, self-assurance, and intelligent.

Creative thinking

This process involves reaching beyond what is normal to solve problems and make decisions. It requires forming new ideas, vision, conceptuality, innovative, imagination, and ingenious. Let us use Ms. Johnson's example, again. On hearing about her complaint, the manager may want to know how many people and in her party. If she says she has four, and there are no tables for four people, the manager may want to know if she is willing to split her party in two, and be seated on two different two-tops. If she says yes, the problem is resolved. Leaders using this process are bright-minded, brilliant, vivid, and dazzling.

Certainly, there are times for using the above mentioned traditional modes of thinking. Many organizations do not succeed because they do not know the right time to think within and outside the box. Some leaders are poor managers of talents that they allow those talents to rust by not thinking intuitively or creatively by developing those talents. One way to release the juice and energy of the workforce is by inviting them and selling your organization's vision, creating an environment that encourages creative thinking and risk taking, and having a good reward and incentive system. Get out of the normal and traditional mode of problem solving and consider using the following modes:

Divergent thinking

This type of thinking is very different from the norm. This process allows you to think away from the usual way and look at a refreshing and more effective way of solving problem and making decision. For instance, your guests are complaining about long wait in the restaurant, giving them free appetizers or drinks to please them maybe costly. A divergent thinking manager may decide to reduce these guests perception by finding something that will occupy their time and minds. This may include providing information about the hotel or restaurant in the waiting area, providing company newsletter, newspaper and magazines, area attractions or other dining facilities. Or if they have children, provide coloring papers. This option may reduce the perception more effectively and less expensive than the first alternative.

Janusian thinking

If you want to kindle you thinking process, use Janusian thinking. This process is based on the Roman deity, Janus. Janus is believed to have two faces in his head, looking at both directions. This is an individual's ability to look at both sides of an issue before making any decisions. Looking at both sides of an issue offers an insight into any conflict, qualms, ambiguity, and hiding assumptions that may existing underneath the surface that the individual may not see. Practicing Janusian thinking, you may ask yourself, what will it cost me if I do not reduce the guests waiting perceptions? What will it cost me by providing some activities for them to perform while waiting? Combining the two questions maybe to ask: how can I minimize the guest wait perception by maximizing the opportunity available to me?

Innovative thinking

To be innovative, you must be original by thinking beyond the normal realm of possibilities. You cannot accept things the way they are, but looking for a novelty way of solving problems. There was a time the foodservice industry with the belief that if you provide good food, people will return. These days the trend is different. A good number of people go out because of good service, because they know that there is no restaurant out there that will deliberately provide tasteless food for its customers. The trend nowadays includes dietary needs, personal and professional chefs, restaurant take-outs, and gourmet coffee. How innovative are you in thinking ahead of your competitors?

Cross training

In all my experience in the hospitality industry, I have not seen the perfect solution to one problem that I believe beseech managers: back and front of the house conflict. The only way this problem could be resolved effectively, is cross-training every front of the house employee in the back, and back of the house employee in the front. This way, everyone will be looking at their new roles from the perspective of the other. At the end of the process, the leader may want the employees to write five to 10 statements about their experiences. And, to explain how the employees can best understand each other. This process will result in a better working relationship.

Some managers assume their role with little training in decision making. Having the power and authority as a manager, you are required to make decisions that will affect the employees and motivate them, make the guests or customers happy so that they will return, and smooth running of the department. Using the following six-steps listed below, will certainly enhance your decision making process.

Define the problem

The first thing to do here is state the exact problem and objectives you wish to achieve. The objective is the results that you expect by making the decision. It should also include any company rules, policies, or procedures that must be taken into consideration while assessing the problem. If your goal is to train George as a front desk agent, your objective should include why is George being trained, what is he suppose to learn, who is to train him, when should the training take place, and how to train him.

Analyze the problem

In analyzing the problem, you gather all the necessary data, facts, or information that will assist you in the decision-making process. In defining the problem, you have outlined the why, what, who, when and how. The next thing is to answer all the questions at this stage. If George is a new employee, why you need to train him is for him to learn and know the front office duties. The next thing is to list what he is suppose to learn; who is suppose to train him (usually the departmental trainer), or whomever the manager chooses; when to train him, usually at a slower period or a more convenient time; and all the tools necessary to do the training. These may include all the paper works involve, computer, pen and papers, and so on.

Develop alternatives

At this stage, you have gathered all the facts and analyze the problem; it is time you put your imaginations to work. You have to brainstorm on alternatives to your why, what, who, when and how, should anything go wrong. While you maybe confident in your why, what, and how, you may not be confident with others. You will want to have a back-up trainer should your original trainer decides not to show up for work. The time you choose to do the training may happen to be the wrong time due to business needs and necessities, which means you may have to reschedule.

Selective the best alternatives

Selecting the best alternative will require some analysis. You must analyze the timing, risks, economy, feasibility, and return on investment. You must also figure whether moving a star employee to train a new employee will affect guest service. And finally, you must go back to your objective to make sure everything you have done to this point meets your objective.

Implement

Now that you have decided on what to do, pass it on to your people and let them execute the actions, and return to your role as a coach. Your decision must be communicated to everyone because this is more or less a delegation. Everyone selected must accept and commit to completing their parts with excellence. Each must fully understand what is at stake and how the decisions they make could affect the new employee and the organization. You must also stress the importance of training new employee the proper way and procedure. There should be no short cut about it.

Continuous improvement

At the end of the training, you will want to get feedback from the new employee and the trainer(s). Their insights and input will help in the improvement process. This will also allow you to evaluate your decision making process, ask a few questions. First of all, did the training meet the objective? Did I cover the entire basis? Did I make the right decisions? Such self-analysis should help you to develop your decision making skills and build your self-confidence.

Problem solving is not just making a choice; it requires an additional step which is the identification of the causes of a problem, and the development of corrective actions. Usually, you become acquainted with a problem by an individual that experiences the problem. Guests complain about bad service; customers complain about bad food; guest complains about dirty room upon check-in, two conflicting employees, and so on. That is to say that, there is a gap between what is suppose to be the standard and what is being provided. The way to solve such problem is as follows:

Describe the problem

You should describe and write down a problem as you see it. That description should also include whatever you believe is causing the problem, and possible problems that may occur as a result of the problem. For example, guests are complaining about waiting too long before getting their food. Such a problem could be causing the guest to be on happy; that unhappiness could lead to the guest not tipping very well, you now have unhappy wait staff, the guest may be leaving your restaurant unhappy, and may not return in the future.

Get the facts

To effectively solve this problem, you have to gather all the relevant facts: that is the why, what, who, when and how. This includes getting the sides of the servers, cooks, expediters, food-runners, and anyone else involve in the service process. May be on your next shift, you will decide to watch everyone as they interact with each other when the restaurant is opened. Your observation of the employees and the operations may help you determine where the communication break down is occurring.

Identify the actual problem and set objectives

In the getting all the facts, you find out that the food is prepared on time, but your runners are slow in the delivery of the food. Now that you have identified the actual problem, set your objective. Your objective maybe you want to keep your runners because they have the right attitude and are willing to listen and learn. Your objective is to reduce that gap between when the food is ready and when it is delivered to the guests. So, you decide to train your runners on the importance of time and how guests perceive waiting for their foods while in the restaurant.

Identify alternative solutions

You generate alternative solutions just as in decision making process.

Select the best solutions and prioritize

Here, you also select the best solution based on your preferences.

Implement solution and Follow-up

You implement your solution and have a follow-up. As you continue to monitor your decision, improve what is working and change what is not.

"Intellectuals solve problems,
geniuses prevent them."
Albert Einstein

Solving problems is a daily practice managers in this industry will do on a day-to-day, if not an hourly basis. You are either faced with employees' problems or guests' problems. Whichever problem we encounter, using logic and common sense approach will certainly be the best way to solve the problem. There is no cookie-cutter approach to any problem solving. The situation may determine the process you will take to solve the problem and make the necessary decision. The result of the decision you make will conclude if you have taken the right decision or not.

Analyze the problem
Continuous improvement
Creative thinking
Cross training
Define the problem
Describe the problem
Develop alternatives
Divergent thinking
Get the facts
Identify alternative solutions
Identify the actual problem and set objectives
Implement
Implement solution and Follow-up
Impulsive thinking
Innovative thinking
Intuitive thinking
Janusian thinking
Rational thinking
Select the best solutions
Selective the best alternatives

1. List the steps in decision-making and problem solving. What are the differences?
2. Which of the thinking processes do you think is most effective? Which do you often use?
3. What is the difference between defining a problem and describing a problem?
4. Why is win-win problem solving important?
5. What are the differences between intuitive and impulsive thinking?

6. Why is it important to get the facts when making a decision?
7. In problem solving, is it always necessary to go through all the steps? Why?
8. In decision making, is it always necessary to go through all the steps? Why?
9. What challenges do you think managers face when making uninformed decision?
10. What is your decision making style?

CHAPTER NINE

The 360 Degree Leader

*"The leader is one who mobilizes others toward
a goal shared by leaders and followers...
Leaders, followers and goals make up the three
equally necessary supports for leadership."*
Gary Wills

What makes an effective leader? How do we know if an effective leader is born or made? Why are some managers better leaders, and others are not? Madsen (2005) asserts that "incompetent bosses, poor managers, and lousy leaders are easy to identify when you work for one" (p. 34). However, trying to measure what makes some effective and others ineffective aren't as simple. But employees know when they are respected, contented, rewarded, appreciated, work is satisfying and gratifying, their leaders is on top of his/her game.

As discussed in chapter one, though the term manager and leadership are used interchangeably, they are very different. According to Madsen (2005), while managers are tactical, recognizing, understanding, and utilizing employee difference to maximize individual performance. Leaders are strategic and conceptualizing a vision for the future by putting employees in teams/groups with the objective for accomplishing organization goals. Your leadership effectiveness could be measured by the attitude and performance of those you lead. Measure your leadership effectiveness by review the 10 measures below.

How to be a better boss:
10 measures of effective managers and leaders

1. A great boss is accessible.
2. A great boss develops healthy relationships with employees.
3. A great boss customizes his/her approach for individuals.
4. A great boss recognizes accomplishments and issues praise regularly.
5. A great boss coaches employees and addresses under-performers.
6. A great boss delegates work and trusts employees to use the skills/strengths they were hired for.
7. A great boss is a great communicator (and listener).
8. A great boss has vision and the ability to rally individuals or teams.
9. A great boss leads by example.
10. A great boss is ethical.

Source: Madsen, J. (2005). How to be a better boss: 10 measures of effective managers and leaders. *Buildings*, 99 (8), 34-36.

Different managers pull strength and knowledge from different directions. Effective leaders pull strength and resiliency from their employees because the serve them and believe in their talent and commitment. Sample (2002) believes that leaders should the first supporter to your employees. By recognizing them as an integral part of your team and seeing them as your colleagues, you set an example of the leadership style that will be readily embraced in your organization.

Leadership traits are different among individuals. The key is to assess your organization and do a self analysis to find your niche. However, listed below are 12 traits that could be applied in any organization culture.

Have a vision

Vision is where you want to be in the future. Think of someone like Walt Disney. His dream was to build a park where parents could take their children, and enjoy the moment, also. See what has become of the simple vision today? The Walt Disney World resort is the number one tourist destination in the world. What about Horst Schulze, formerly of Ritz-Carlton? A member of the team who developed the Ritz-Carlton philosophy of "Ladies and Gentlemen serving Ladies and Gentlemen." Under his leadership, Ritz-Carlton won the Malcolm Baldridge National Quality Award in 1992 and again in 1999. Ritz-Carlton is the first and only service organization to win the coveted award two times. It is so because of this simple question: "what is vision without the passion to see it through?"

Communicate: Listen to learn

Communication is one of the hall marks of a great leader. The key to effective communication is adjusting your communication style according to the needs of the situation. That is, be aware of your emotions, tones, body language, metaphors, keeping the communication simple, encourage one-on-one communication, and repeating yourself as often as possible. The more succinct you communicate organization goal and vision, the more your employees will rally around you. Do not only listen to what the employees are saying, listen with the intent on understanding where they are coming from. If an employee is expressing her frustration about the system, and you are concern about the customer's reaction, you are not listening to the employee. The employees need your full and undivided attention, recognize their needs.

Open-door policy

Several people say they have an open door policy, but are never available when they are needed. As a leader, you must be available and visible to the employees. Employee access to you should be possible at all times. The employees should be free to enter your office and discuss anything of interest or concern with you, without fear or favor, and also have the confidence that whatever the nature of the discussion, it will be kept confidential. In the hospitality industry, frontline managers should be accessible to the employees in the operations.

Employees are number "One"

In the hustling and bustling of the hospitality industry, some managers forget about the employees and concentrate on satisfying the guests. This is the job of the employees. Your job is to make your employees happy. The first step to accomplishing this is by making your employee number one. They are in the front lines of the operations and interact with the guest and customers more often and on a daily basis than you. Treat the employees very well, listen to their concerns, solve everyday problems they may have, keep open the line of communication, praise them when they do a good job and discuss any area of improvement, then sit back and let them do their work. You will be amazed how good, effective and efficient the operation runs with little assistance from you. You have less grey hair and lower blood pressure.

The top 10 communication traits of effective leaders

1. Employees are number one
2. Get into the trenches
3. Follow through on feedback
4. Be up-front with difficult news

5. Deliver meaningful measures
6. Be authentic
7. Check in often
8. Right message, right medium
9. Recognize others
10. Keep listening

Source: Dulye, L. (2004). The top 10 communication traits of effective leaders. *Leadership Communication*, 5 (4), 10-11.

It is about "we," not "me or I"

If you are a manager that always want you ideas and opinion to be the order of the day, you really have a problem. If you are a manager that likes to take center stage, you really have a bigger problem. If you are a manager that likes to take credit and apportion blame, you are dead on arrival (DOA). It is always about *"we,"* not *"me or I."* Include everyone in the process, communicate with everyone, talk to everyone, and take responsibility for failure because you are at the head, and give everyone credit for success because they performed excellently under your supervision. Leadership is all about "we" not "me" or "I."

> "Leadership is an opportunity to serve. It is not a trumpet call to self-importance."
> – J. Donald Walters

Empower and delegate

While micromanagement is a way of keeping control and ensuring the completion of tasks, it is rarely effective. Employees like an environment where trust and motivation is part of the norm. Employees are more dedicated when you empower them to make decision within their job description. You cannot be everywhere at all times, empower your employees to make certain decisions. Neither can you carry out all your responsibilities without your employees. Select, train, develop and delegate some of your tasks. You cannot be at the front desk, gift shop, or the restaurant every time. So, it is wise to delegate some of your tasks to individuals you have identified as competent. Effective delegation allows you to have time for other important things. Leaders that do not trust their employees enough to empower and delegate tasks might be failing to capitalize on the employees' valuable talents, opinions, and ideas. Chapter five offered several ways to empower and delegate effectively.

Exude energy

Effective leaders explode with energy, because it is contagious on their employees. This is one of the ways to show optimism and determination. Your followers will commit to you if you have confidence in yourself, and you show that confidence in their abilities. Show your appreciation honestly, acknowledge good performance promptly, recognize positive actions instantly, and do your job like a "wounded lion." When you depart, the employees will sing your praise, some may follow you wherever you go because of your positive energy and attitude.

Must have honesty, integrity, and ethics

"Think of integrity as having your insides match your outside. When your behavior is consistent with your values, they are integrated" (Carbone, 1996, p. 28). To earn the honor of the employees, you have to develop a sense of integrity, credibility, trust, and motivate people to follow your vision. In being honest, you must deal with people in transparently, with consistency, with openness, and truthfully. Ethically, think before acting. It is your deeds and actions that speak volume. With companies such as ENRON and WorldCom, employees are suspicious of their leaders. Being ethical is not only politically correct; it is the right thing to be.

Praise, praise, and praise

The old adage says "you can catch more bees with honey than vinegar." This is very true. If you praise your employees' positive performance on a regular basis, you will spend less time correcting or motivating them. Praising and saying thank you for a job well done, cost you nothing and cannot be measured in any monetary form. If you do not praise, you will lose a good employee, and the cost of hiring a replacement can be measured in monetary ways. McCrarey (2005) says that "praising positive actions yields more positive results and makes it easier to lead workers to improved performance" (p. 54). More so, do not forget the rule of thumb for discipline: praise in public, reprimand in private.

Identify your replacement

In every organization, there are always those employees that put in over 100 percent performance. Amongst them is this particular individual who turns in an A-plus production, and consistently turn in great performance each and every time. You certainly know and recognize this employee. This is your replacement. The first thing you want to do is "figure out what motivates your star and try to offer more of it" (Fisher, 2004, p. 70).

Leadership skill clusters

Leadership drivers "core skills"	Leadership support skills	Results/Effects of good leadership
• Self-Awareness • Articulate the vision • Goal setting & planning	• Delegation, feedback & control • Time management/ Self management • Problem solving • Decision making	• Conflict management • Team building • Motivating & Influencing • Stress management

Source: Zornada, M. (2005). Defining the skills of a leader. *British Journal of Administrative Management*, 49, 18-19.

Involve others in decision making

Everyone feels important. You as a leader want to make all the people that work for you feel more important than they may perceive. One way to do this is by involving them in decision making process. Solicit their inputs, ideas as much as possible. They will feel special, and perceive that you count on them in times of decision making. More importantly, give credit to everyone and have the humility to admit when you are wrong. It requires a lot of humility to admit mistakes. Your employees will respect and admire you more when you exercise this humility.

Recognize, reward excellence, and celebrate success

As you lead the employees, be aware of their strength and areas of development. At the same time, recognize the talented employees and reward them for their excellence work and dedication. Celebrate every success as the employees improve their skills, potentials and education. Also, recognize their employment and wedding anniversaries, and birthdays. No recognition or celebration is too small or too big, as they are all forms of motivating and encouraging the employees.

Human Relations
The six most important words: "I
admit I made a mistake."
The five most important words: "You did a good job."
The four most important words:
"What is your opinion."
The three most important words: "If you please."
The two most important words: "Thank you,"
The one most important word: "We"
The least most important word: "I"
Author: Unknown

Source: http://www.nwlink.com/~donclark/leader/leadcon.html

Leadership is one of the facets of management; and becoming an effective leader is what distinguishes you from every other manager. Most leaders have leadership traits that fit their personality and their organizational culture. You may have your own style that fits you and does not contradict your organizational culture and norms. The key to being an effective leader is recognizing the needs of people and working to meet them. If you take care of your employees, they will take care of your guests and you do not have to worry about the bottom line: it will be looking profitable.

Involve the employees in as many decisions as possible. Take their suggestion and opinions and act on them, it will make them feel important. Practice what you preach, walk around with a big stick and say little. Demonstrate your social intelligent skills. The employees will remember you for your actions rather than for your words, because actions speak volume. Remember, leadership is not a popularity contest. It is about doing the right thing; and effective leaders *do the right things right*.

Celebrate success
Decision making
Delegate
Empower
Ethics
Exude energy
Have a vision
Honesty
Identify your replacement
Integrity
Listen to learn
Open-door policy
Praise
Recognize
Reward

1. What is your understanding of a 360 degree leader?
2. Why is it important to celebrate the employees' successes?
3. Why is praise necessary?
4. Why do you think human relation is a necessary skill for leaders?
5. What are the differences between "doing the right thing" and "doing the right things right?"
6. What leadership traits are important to you?
7. Why do you think it is important to include the employees in decision-making process?
8. How would getting employees involved in decision-making process motivate them and improve their productivity?
9. Do you believe in open-door policy? What are its advantages and disadvantages?
10. What do you think it is meant by "employees are number one?"

References

Alexander, L. (1997). Leaders know how to listen. *HR Focus,* 74 (94), 25.

Aquila, A. J., (2004). The eternal riddle of being an effective leader. *Accounting Today,* 8-9.

Baytos, L. M. (1995). Task forces drive successful diversity efforts. *HR Magazine,* 40(10), 95-98.

Bendick, M. Jr., Egan, M. L., and Lofhjelm, S. M. (2001). Workforce diversity training:

From anti-discrimination compliance to organizational development. *Human Resources Development,* 24 (2), 10-25.

Bowman, R. F. (2005). Teachers as servant leaders. The Clearing House, 78 (60), 257-259.

Carbonet, L. (1996). Integrity, courage, and vision: The marks of a leader. Nation's Restaurant News, 30 (15), 28.

Clark, D. (1997). The art and science of leadership: Concepts of leadership. Retrieved on April 25, 2006. Available online: http://www.nwlink.com/~donclark/leader/leader.html

DeVito, J. A. (2004). *The interpersonal communication book* (10ᵗʰ ed). Upper Saddle River, NJ: Prentice Hall, Inc.

DeVoe, D. (1999). Management tips from an expert. *InfoWorld,* 21(44), 79.

Drummond, K. E. (1990). *Human resources management for the hospitality industry.* New York, N.Y.: John Wiley & Sons, Inc.

Dulye, L. (2004). The top 10 communication traits of effective leaders. *Leadership Communication,* 5 (4), 10-11.

Emmerich, R. (2005). Follow the 10 commandments of employee motivation. *Des Moine Business Record,* 23 (20), 26-27.

Evenson, R. (1998). How to effectively deal with a poor performer: Your true test of leadership. *Supervision,* 59(7), 12-14.

Fisher, A. (2004). Turn star employees into superstars. *Fortune,* 150 (12), 70.

Goodwin, C., Squire III, A. B., and Chapman, E. (2005). *"The hospitality supervisor's survival kit."* Upper Saddle River, NJ: Prentice Hall, Inc.

Iverson, K. M. (2001). *Managing human resources in the hospitality industry: An experiential approach.* Upper Saddle River, NJ: Prentice Hall, Inc.

Kello, J. (2005). Don't train employees in a silo: Think "outside the classroom" for better results. *Industrial Safety & Hygiene News,* 30 (10), 22-25.

Kerfoot, K. (2004). On leadership: 'In your corner' leadership. *Urologic Nursing,* 24 (4), 357-358.

Knight, C. F. and Dyer, D. (2005). Ten traits of effective leaders. *Harvard Management Update,* 10 (10), 3-6.

Madsen, J. (2005). How to be a better boss: 10 measures of effective managers and leaders. *Buildings,* 99 (8), 34-36.

Marzano, W. A., (2005). Motivating and energizing your team: 10 tips for success, *Academic Leader,* 21 (5), 4-5.

McCrarey, S. (2005). Motivating the workforce with a positive culture: Recognition that works. *Franchising World,* 37 (3), 54-58.

Miller, J. E., Walker, J. R., & Drummond, K. E. (2007). *Supervision in the hospitality industry,* (5th ed.). Hoboken, NJ: John Willey & Sons.

Nahavandi, A. (2006). *The art and science of leadership,* (4th ed.). Upper Saddle River, NJ: Prentice Hall, Inc.

National Restaurant Association (2005). *2005 restaurant industry fact sheet.* Washington, DC; National Restaurant Association. (2003) Radisson training initiative. *Business Travel World,* 34.

Richard, O. C. (2000). Racial diversity, business strategy, and firm performance: A resource-based view. *Academy of Management Journal,* 43(2), 164-173.

Robbins, S. P., & Hunsaker, P. L. (2007). *Training in interpersonal skills: Tips for managing people at work* (4th. Ed.). Upper Saddle River, NJ: Prentice Hall, Inc.

Rowe, R. (2003). Leaders as servants. *New Zealand Management, 50*(1), 24.

Salomon, M. F., & Schork, J. M. (2003). Turn diversity to your advantage. *Research Technology Management*, 46(4), 37-44.

Sample, S. (2002). *The contrarian's guide to leadership.* New York: Jossey-Bass.

Schramm, J. (2003). Acting affirmatively. *HR Magazine,* 48(9), 192.

Scott, M. (2000). 7 pitfalls for managers when handling poor performers and how to overcome them. *Manage,*

Soni, V. (2000). A twenty-first-century reception for diversity in the public sector: A case study. *Public Administrator Review, 60(5), 395-408. Review,* 74(5), 79-81.

Schwartz, A. E. (1995). Counseling the marginal performer. CPA Journal, 65(2), 66-67.

Tesone, D. V. (2005). *Human resources management in the hospitality industry: A practitioner's perspective.* Upper Saddle River, NJ: Prentice Hall, Inc.

Tesone, D. V. (2005). *Supervision skills for the service industry: How to do it.* Upper Saddle River, NJ: Prentice Hall, Inc.

The Holy Bible, New King James Version (1982). Nashville, TN: Thomas Nelson Publishers.

Von Bergen, C. W., & Soper, B. (2002). Unintended negative effects of diversity management. *Public Personnel Management*, 31(2), 239-241.

Zornada, M. (2005). Defining the skills of a leader. *British Journal of Administrative Management,* 49, 18-19.

www.ingramcontent.com/pod-product-compliance
Lightning Source LLC
Chambersburg PA
CBHW020239290526
45784CB00003B/1038